Contents

Part C: Reference section

Grammar

for Teachers

The essential guide
to how English works

JOHN SEELY

Published by Oxpecker
PO Box 134
Tiverton
EX16 0AR
United Kingdom
info@oxpecker.co.uk
+44 (0)1884 881 553

First published 2006

Revised 2007

ISBN 13: 978-0-9553451-2-8

ISBN 10: 0-9553451-2-X

Editorial work by Carolyn Richardson Publishing Services

Cover design by Oxpecker

Book design and typesetting by Oxpecker

Set in Adobe Myriad Pro, GFY Jeanna, and ITC Officina Sans

About this book

Grammar for Teachers has been written for teachers who need an understanding of the structure of English for their work. It is particularly suitable for those teaching English to students aged 8–15. It will also be valuable for those preparing to teach modern foreign languages and English as an additional or foreign language.

There has been considerable argument about the value of teaching English grammar to students whose first language is English. There can be little doubt, however, that their teachers should have a grasp of the structure of English and of the terminology used to describe it. In saying this, I am using the word 'grammar' in a strict sense. You will not find any explanations of terms from punctuation, spelling, vocabulary, or literary criticism here.

Not only are terms explained; they are also placed in their grammatical context. Glossaries that simply explain what a term means are useful for a quick check. However they are much more useful if they also enable you to see how that grammatical feature fits into the whole pattern. That is what this book does.

But I must add a note of caution. This is a descriptive grammar. It describes how English is used. It does not tell you how you ought to use it. I have followed the grammatical description established by major authorities such as Quirk and Greenbaum. (The books to which I have referred are listed on page 155 under 'Further reading'.) That said, I cannot be held responsible for the results of any conflict that might arise between the interpretation of grammar set down in this book and that offered by any local or national curriculum or syllabus.

I hope you find Grammar for Teachers helpful in your work as a teacher. Please contact me c/o Oxpecker if there are things you think should be in the book and aren't – or if there are areas where the explanations are not as clear as you would like. There are contact details on page 4.

John Seely

About the author

John Seely was a teacher and lecturer for almost 25 years before giving up the day job to become a full-time author. He taught English and drama in schools and colleges in England, Scotland, Indonesia, and Kenya, at all levels from primary to postgraduate. Now, as well as his work as a writer and editor, he gives workshops and seminars on language and communication skills in Britain and overseas.

John's books are used all over the world. His first title was a book for teachers about language and drama, *In Context,* published in 1976. There followed a stream of successful textbooks, such as *Oxford Secondary English*, *The Oxford English Programme*, and *The Heinemann English Programme*. Over the past fifteen years he has written a range of books about language and communication skills. These include *The Oxford Guide to Effective Writing and Speaking*, *Everyday Grammar*, and the *Oxford A–Z of Grammar and Punctuation*. He is Series Editor of the *Heinemann Shakespeare* and *Heinemann Advanced Shakespeare* series.

He is a former Chair of the Authors' Licensing and Collecting Society and director of the Copyright Licensing Agency.

John lives in Devon, in the South-West of England, with his wife Elizabeth.

About the 2007 edition

I have taken the opportunity of this revised edition to correct a few errors that had crept in to the first printing. I have also changed some of the examples, replacing a number of British English quotations with texts from North America and elsewhere around the world.

JS

Introduction

A look at what grammar is and how this book approaches the subject. How readers with different levels of knowledge can use the book: from absolute beginners to those who just need a quick refresher course.

Grammar for Teachers provides a clear, simple and systematic approach to understanding the structure of English. It shows how words are built up into phrases which form parts of clauses, and how clauses are combined into sentences.

Grammar for Teachers is designed to be used by three groups of readers:

❑ Those who are new to grammar and want to 'begin at the beginning'.

❑ Readers who know something about grammar and want to improve their knowledge and/or fill in the gaps.

❑ Users who know some grammar but wish to look up particular grammatical terms.

To fulfil these aims, the book is in three parts:

❑ **Part A: Overview**
Chapters 2–6 explain the basics of English grammar. They introduce the four main levels: word, phrase, clause, and sentence, and show how they fit together. They do this by using very simple examples which are gradually developed into bigger and more complex structures. In this part of the book some of the examples (mainly in Chapter 2) are invented to avoid unnecessary complication. However, most of the examples are from real texts.

❑ **Part B: The details**
Chapters 7–10 build on the foundation provided by Part A. They explore the four main levels in some detail, beginning with words. With a very small number of exceptions, the text is illustrated by real life examples, so that you can see genuine language at work.

❑   **Part C: Reference section**
All the technical terms used in the book are explained in detail in the Glossary. This contains all the grammatical terms that are necessary for a proper understanding of grammar. All the illustrative examples in the Glossary are taken from real-life texts from around the world.

This section also includes a list of Further Reading and the Index.

What sort of grammar?

The word 'grammar' is much abused. So it is worth setting out what this book does – and does not – mean by it. By 'grammar' I mean the description of the ways in which English words are combined to form meaningful and acceptable sentences. In technical terms this means:

❑   SYNTAX: the systematic rules by which we group and order words to form phrases, clauses, and sentences.

❑   MORPHOLOGY: the ways in which the forms of words are changed according to their use in phrases, clauses, and sentences.

This limited definition leaves out a lot of things some people include in their broader use of 'grammar'. It does **not** include:

❑   spelling

❑   punctuation

❑   how texts larger than sentences are constructed

❑   style.

More important, perhaps, it is not concerned with what speakers and writers *should* and *should not* do with their language. In other words the approach is solidly descriptive rather than prescriptive.

Approach
A descriptive approach to grammar begins with real language and sets out the patterns that can be seen in it. Descriptive grammar sets out the rules by which phrases, clauses, and sentences are

constructed by real people in real situations. 'Rules' here means 'patterns' and not 'laws that must be obeyed'. In everyday life there is a rich variety in the way that people use language to communicate. The real language I have used for illustrations has been taken from a wide variety of genuine written and spoken texts. Inevitably when we try to describe the patterns of that usage we tend to simplify. The way we use language is creative and subtle. When we try to pin down usage there are always examples that 'don't fit the rules'. This short book is simply a starting point for those who wish to begin to understand how English works. If you feel you need more detail there is a list of Further Reading on page 155.

Using this book

As I said earlier, how you use this book depends on your starting point. If you aren't sure, then begin with Part A; you will soon find out whether this is the right place or whether you can move on to Part B. At each point you will find cross-reference boxes which will direct you to pages where more information can be found on related topics. For example:

☐ to describe a WORD CLASS

☐ to describe a CLAUSE ELEMENT

Verbs as a word class

In this sense, verbs are on the same level as NOUNS, ADJECTIVES and ADVERBS.

Verbs as words are described in more detail in Chapter 7.

One of the key features of verbs is that they change their form, or INFLECT more than other words.

Verb inflection

And whenever a word appears in SMALL CAPS you will find a detailed explanation of its meaning in the Glossary.

Further help

There is a companion web site for this book:

http://www.grammarforteachers.com

This contains additional materials (including a downloadable 92-page *Workbook)*, details of new publications, and information about my programmae of grammar workshops.

I should like to make both book and website as helpful and interactive as possible. Both will be updated as frequently as practicable to take account of readers' questions, criticisms and suggestions. (By using print-on-demand technology I can bring out revised editions of the printed book much more frequently and economically than is the case with conventional means.) Please use the response form on the web site, or write to me using the contact details below. If your comments lead to a significant change to the book, then you will be entitled to receive the revised edition free of charge.

John Seely

Oxpecker
PO Box 134
Tiverton
EX16 0AR
United Kingdom

phone: +44 (0)1884 881 553

email: john@oxpecker.co.uk

PART A

Overview

Seven amazing facts about elephants

All the possible sentences in English are built up from only seven different patterns of clause. Once you know how to use those seven patterns you can make literally millions of different sentences.

Levels

Grammar works at several different levels:

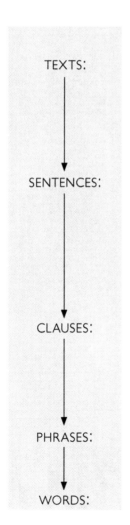

TEXTS:	*Then an elephant trumpeted, and they all took it up for five or ten terrible seconds. The dew from the trees above spattered down like rain on the unseen backs, and a dull booming noise began, not very loud at first, and Little Toomai could not tell what it was.*

SENTENCES:	*Then an elephant trumpeted, and they all took it up for five or ten terrible seconds.*	*The dew from the trees above spattered down like rain on the unseen backs, and a dull booming noise began, not very loud at first, and Little Toomai could not tell what it was.*

CLAUSES:	*The dew from the trees above spattered down like rain on the unseen backs*	*a dull booming noise began, not very loud at first*	*Little Toomai could not tell*	*what it was*

PHRASES:	*The dew from the trees above*	*spattered*	*down*	*like rain*

WORDS:	*The*	*dew*	*from*	*the*

In English curriculum documents the main emphasis is on words and sentences, but, as you can see from the example opposite, it is tricky to jump straight from word to SENTENCE without the intervening steps of clauses and phrases. How the four levels work together should become clearer as you work through Part A, and it is spelt out in more detail in Part B.

Sentences

Grammar is about how sentences are constructed. Sentences, however, are not easy to define. One traditional definition is that a sentence is 'the expression of a complete thought or idea'. However, it is not difficult to think of sentences that are grammatically correct, but which do not fit this definition. For example, it would be difficult to explain the complete thought or idea in:

> *Is that it?*

Equally, there are plenty of non-sentences that do seem to express a complete thought or idea. For example:

> *DANGER LIVE CURRENT*

or

> *God*

And then again, you have to remember that it is perfectly possible to construct sentences that are grammatically acceptable, but which don't make a lot of sense. Chomsky's famous example of this was *Colorless green ideas sleep furiously*.

So it is better to define a sentence in formal terms as a grammatical unit that consists of one or more FINITE CLAUSES.

Sentences are covered in detail in Chapter 10.

Sentence types
There are four types of sentence:

❏ DECLARATIVE
   These are sentences normally used to make statements such as *Elephants are dangerous*.

❏ INTERROGATIVE
   These are normally used to ask questions like *Are elephants dangerous?* or *What are those elephants doing?*

❑   IMPERATIVE

These are normally used to make commands, orders, and requests, like *Look at that elephant!*

❑   EXCLAMATIVE

These are used to make exclamations of various kinds such as *How charming that little baby elephant is!*

Each of these sentence types has a distinctive word order. In this chapter, which is all about word order, we shall stick to declarative sentences (the type used to make statements) since they are by far the most common.

Five basic clause patterns

Sentences are covered in detail in Chapter 10.

Throughout this chapter we'll look at sentences that consist of just one clause (see SIMPLE SENTENCE) and in the process find out more about what a clause actually is. We'll do this by looking at sentences no more than four words long.

As the chapter title suggests, all the sample sentences are about elephants. If you want to try out the ideas and sentence patterns in the chapter, think of a topic of your own as the basis for parallel sentences. Choose a PLURAL CONCRETE NOUN (one that refers to a person, place, or thing) – like *books, trains,* or *teachers*. Then use it to construct sentences with the same patterns as the *elephant* ones used as examples.

Subject + verb

The shortest sentence you can make starting with the word *elephants* consists of two words. For example:

Elephants exist.

This sentence consists of one clause. The clause has two parts, a SUBJECT and a VERB:

SUBJECT	VERB
Elephants	*exist.*

The subject

The subject of a simple sentence:

❑ comes at or near the beginning of the sentence

❑ comes before the verb

❑ is a NOUN or 'a noun-like thing'

❑ often gives a good idea of what the sentence is going to be about.

> 'Noun-like things' are explored in Chapter 3.

The verb

The verb of a simple sentence:

❑ normally comes immediately or shortly after the subject

❑ AGREES with the subject:

- in NUMBER
  One elephant walks; two elephants walk.

- in PERSON
  I am; she is; they are

❑ provides information about an action (*talks*) or a state (*believes*) or links the subject to another part of the sentence in some other way (as *am* does in the sentence *I am happy.*)

The simple pattern of SUBJECT + VERB can be used to generate thousands of sentences. They may have just two words like the sample sentence, or they may have many more:

SUBJECT	VERB
Elephants	*exist.*
The older bull elephants	*are beginning to stampede.*
A few more trainees	*will have departed.*

Although the last two sentences have many more words than the first, they still have the same two clause elements: subject and verb. In the next chapter we'll look at how a single noun like *Elephants* can build into a group of words like *The older bull elephants*. Chapter 4 looks at verbs in a similar way.

Subject + verb + object

You can't, of course, make sentences of the SUBJECT + VERB type with just any old verb. This is not a complete sentence:

  Elephants like ✗

The immediate response to that is: 'like what?' The sentence is missing a key part: the object. So our second pattern covers sentences like this:

SUBJECT	VERB	OBJECT	
Elephants	*like*	*grass.*	

The object

The OBJECT of a clause or sentence:

- ❑ normally comes after the verb
- ❑ is a noun or 'noun-like thing'
- ❑ usually refers to a different person, thing or idea from the subject. (The exception to this is objects that include the part-word *-self*, as in *I cut myself*, where subject and object refer to the same person.)
- ❑ very often tells us about a person or thing that is
  - affected by the action of the verb, **or**
  - 'acted upon' in some way.

  In the example, the grass is clearly affected by the action of *eating*.

The SUBJECT + VERB + OBJECT pattern can be lengthened in a similar way to the subject + verb one:

SUBJECT	VERB	OBJECT
Elephants	*like*	*grass.*
An adult bull elephant	*can be expected to eat*	*tons of grass.*
Someone	*might have warned*	*the poor girl.*

Again, the second and third sentences follow exactly the same pattern as the first, even though each has a lot more words.

Subject + verb + object + object

We have seen that some verbs, like *want*, must have an object. A number of verbs,however, usually have not one object, but two. So the 'sentence' below is not complete, even though it has a subject, a verb, and and one object:

    Elephants give children ✘

We are left asking, *Elephants give children* **what**? It is true that *children* is an object, of a kind; it fulfils all the requirements in the list on the previous page. But verbs like *give* need a second object:

SUBJECT	VERB	INDIRECT OBJECT	DIRECT OBJECT	
Elephants	*give*	*children*	*rides.*	✔

Rides is the DIRECT OBJECT – it is what the elephants give. *Children* is the INDIRECT OBJECT because the children are the ones who benefit from the rides – the people that the rides are being given to. You can always tell this type of sentence because it can be rephrased like this:

SUBJECT	VERB	INDIRECT OBJECT	DIRECT OBJECT
Elephants	*give*	*children*	*rides.*

Elephants	*give*	*rides*	*to children.*
SUBJECT	VERB	DIRECT OBJECT	INDIRECT OBJECT

Many verbs that refer to the action of passing something from one person or thing to another work in this way. Examples are *pass* and *show*:

SUBJECT	VERB	INDIRECT OBJECT	DIRECT OBJECT
Henry	passed	her	some thin, crustless brown bread and butter.
He	showed	them	the careful layout of the hospital.

Subject + verb + complement

There is another pattern which resembles the SUBJECT + VERB + OBJECT pattern, but which is actually very different:

SUBJECT	VERB	COMPLEMENT
Elephants	are	animals.

The word *animals* is a 'noun or noun-like thing' and it comes after the verb, so we might expect it to be the object. But it fails the other test: it does not refer to something different from the subject. The items before and after the verb refer to the same thing. The sentence is more like a mathematical equation:

> Elephants = animals.

The complement

In this clause pattern the element that comes after the verb provides more information about the subject, it serves to complete it, so it is called the complement, or more fully, the SUBJECT COMPLEMENT. It:

❑ comes after the verb

❑ is either:

- a NOUN (or 'noun-like thing'), **or**

- an ADJECTIVE (as in the sentence, *Elephants are big.*)

❑ refers to the same person or thing as the subject.

This type of clause uses a special type of verb, called a LINKING (or COPULAR) VERB. The commonest of these is *be*. Others are *become* and *seem*:

SUBJECT	VERB	COMPLEMENT
She	*became*	*a freelance business writer.*
This explanation	*may not seem*	*very attractive.*

Subject + verb + object + complement

Objects, as well as subjects, can have complements. They occur in clauses constructed on the following pattern:

SUBJECT	VERB	OBJECT	OBJECT COMPLEMENT
Elephants	*make*	*children*	*happy.*

You can contrast this clause with one we looked at earlier:

SUBJECT	VERB	INDIRECT OBJECT	DIRECT OBJECT
Elephants	*give*	*children*	*rides.*

It is true that both have two elements after the verb: a direct object and something else. In the earlier sentence, *children* and *rides* refer to completely different things. In this sentence, *children* and *happy* refer to the same thing. The word *happy* serves to give more information about the object, *children*: it completes it. Hence the name OBJECT COMPLEMENT. To use the mathematical analogy, we could represent the sample sentence as:

Elephants make children = happy.

The object complement

This clause element:

❑ comes after the object

❑ provides additional information about the object

❑ can be either:

- a noun (or 'noun-like thing'), as in the sentence *They made me secretary*, **or**

- an adjective, like *happy*.

The story so far

We have now looked at five basic clause patterns:

SUBJECT	VERB		
Elephants	*exist.*		

SUBJECT	VERB	OBJECT	
Elephants	*like*	*grass.*	

SUBJECT	VERB	INDIRECT OBJECT	DIRECT OBJECT
Elephants	*give*	*children*	*rides.*

SUBJECT	VERB	COMPLEMENT	
Elephants	*are*	*animals.*	

SUBJECT	VERB	OBJECT	COMPLEMENT
Elephants	*make*	*children*	*happy.*

In each of these patterns every clause element is essential. If you remove one element the structure stops being a clause and becomes grammatically incomplete.

The missing piece of the jigsaw

There are two other clause patterns which are much less common than the five we have been looking at so far. They only occur with a very small number of verbs, but they are important.

Subject + verb + adverbial

We saw how some verbs need to be followed by particular clause elements. For example, in this pattern:

SUBJECT	VERB	?
Elephants	*like*	_____

we need an object to complete the pattern. Similarly the pattern *Elephants are* _____ needs a complement to complete it. The following sentence opening sets up a similar need:

SUBJECT	VERB	?
Elephants	*live*	———————

This part sentence raises questions such as, *Elephants live* **where**? To complete the pattern we need a third element:

SUBJECT	VERB	ADVERBIAL
Elephants	*live*	*here.*

Verbs that need an ADVERBIAL in this way refer to movement (for example, *hurtle*) or position (for example, *hang*):

SUBJECT	VERB	ADVERBIAL
They	*hurtled*	*across the landing.*
Dauntless's dark wet hair	*was hanging*	*over his eyes.*

Subject + verb + object + adverbial

There is also a small group of verbs that take an object and then also require an adverbial. For example:

SUBJECT	VERB	OBJECT	ADVERBIAL
The elephant	*thrust*	*him*	*away.*

The sentence does not work without *away*. Verbs that usually need an object to be followed by an adverbial include *put* and *throw*:

SUBJECT	VERB	OBJECT	ADVERBIAL
He	*put*	*his face*	*in his hands.*
She	*threw*	*the bottle*	*over towards Cleo's lap.*

Adverbials

So adverbials are the missing piece of the jigsaw, bringing the total number of clause patterns to seven. Unfortunately, as we shall see, adverbials are awkward customers. Although they only crop up in these two 'compulsory' positions in clause patterns, they can appear almost anywhere in any of the other patterns as an optional element:

SUBJECT	VERB	ADVERBIAL	
Elephants	*exist*	*now.*	
SUBJECT	VERB	OBJECT	ADVERBIAL
Elephants	*eat*	*grass*	*slowly.*
ADVERBIAL	SUBJECT	VERB	COMPLEMENT
Usually	*elephants*	*are*	*big.*

Adverbials carry information about when, where, and how the events in the sentence occur.

To sum up: the seven basic clause patterns

SUBJECT	VERB		
Elephants	*exist.*		
SUBJECT	VERB	OBJECT	
Elephants	*like*	*grass.*	
SUBJECT	VERB	INDIRECT OBJECT	DIRECT OBJECT
Elephants	*give*	*children*	*rides.*
SUBJECT	VERB	COMPLEMENT	
Elephants	*are*	*animals.*	
SUBJECT	VERB	OBJECT	COMPLEMENT
Elephants	*make*	*children*	*happy.*
SUBJECT	VERB	ADVERBIAL	
Elephants	*live*	*here.*	
SUBJECT	VERB	OBJECT	ADVERBIAL
The elephant	*thrust*	*him*	*away.*

Nouns and noun-like things

We saw in the previous chapter that the subject, object, or complement of a clause could be a noun...or a 'noun-like thing'. In this chapter we have a closer look at nouns and related grammatical features.

Nouns

Most people have a fairly shrewd idea of what a noun is. Nouns tell us about people places things and ideas. They can be divided into two groups: PROPER nouns and COMMON nouns.

Proper nouns are the names of individual people, places, organisations, works of art, and so forth. The important thing about proper nouns is that they refer to things that are one-off. You can only have one *George Washington* or *Milton Keynes*. We mark this special nature by awarding initial capital letters. When official titles are used in this way we give them a capital letter:

The Hungarian Foreign Minister...

When they aren't, we don't:

...regular consultative meetings of foreign ministers...

Some writers no longer use capital letters in this way, but the convention is still widespread.

All other nouns are common. Some people like to divide common nouns into ABSTRACT and CONCRETE NOUNS, but this is more to do with what they mean than how they behave grammatically. For example, there is little grammatical difference between these concrete nouns:

car   stone   book

and these abstract nouns:

dream   hope   idea.

A more useful way of dividing nouns is into COUNTABLE and UN-COUNTABLE. As the names suggest, countable nouns regularly have a plural form, which usually ends in 's', while uncountable nouns do not. Uncountables include all proper nouns and many (but not all) abstract nouns. For example, you cannot have more than

There is more about COUNTABLE and UNCOUNT-ABLE nouns on pages 48–49.

one *contentment*. There is also a small group of concrete nouns that are usually uncountable, mostly things that are thought of in the mass rather than as a set of individual items: *sand, mud, ice, butter*, and so forth. But beware: almost all uncountables can become countable in special situations. For example:

Sands of time run out for strife-torn factory

You might ask whether it matters if a noun is countable or not. The answer is that certain words cannot be used before un-countable nouns. These are words that describe quantity. They include:

each   several   few   many

Nor can you precede an uncountable with the articles *a* or *an*. More important, it is not standard English to use *less* before a countable plural. It's *less butter* and *fewer biscuits*. But, especially in speech, more and more people are using *less* with plural nouns.

To sum up: nouns can be proper or common, countable or un-countable:

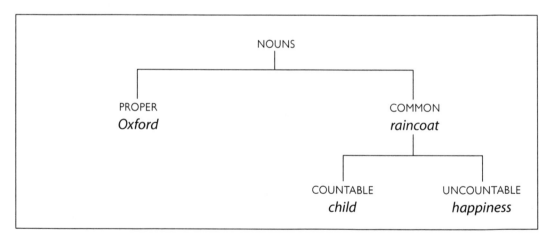

In addition, as we shall see, nouns can be turned into NOUN PHRASES and can be MODIFIED by ADJECTIVES.

Pronouns

There is more about PRONOUNS on pages 64–66.

But before that, there is an important group of words that can also act as the subject, object, or complement of a clause: PRONOUNS. It is sometimes said that they are called ***pro***nouns because they are used *instead of* nouns. This is a rather misleading oversimplification. Look at that last sentence. *This* is definitely a pronoun, but it isn't standing in for a noun. It is referring back to a whole sentence which begins, *It is sometimes said...* So it is more accurate to say that **pronouns refer back to something already written or said**. This may be:

❑ a noun

❑ another pronoun or group of pronouns

❑ a noun phrase (shortly to be explained)

❑ a section of text – part or all of a sentence, or even a group of sentences

❑ an idea or fact already mentioned.

In addition, you will probably have noticed that we sometimes use *it* as the subject of a sentence when it refers back to nothing at all:

It is raining.

In sentences like that, *it* is described as a DUMMY SUBJECT because in effect the sentence has no real subject. *There* can be used in a similar way:

There's a lot of politics involved.

Types of pronoun

Pronouns come in a range of shapes and sizes, according to use. They are covered in more detail in Part B and are listed here for completeness:

TYPE	EXAMPLES	
PERSONAL	*I / me*	*he/him*
POSSESSIVE	*mine*	*hers*
REFLEXIVE	*myself*	*themselves*
DEMONSTRATIVE	*this*	*that*
INDEFINITE	*someone*	*anyone*
INTERROGATIVE	*who*	*what*
RELATIVE	*who*	*that*

Pronouns in use

The best way to get a good hold on how pronouns work is to take that list and read through a piece of prose identifying the different types of pronoun used and the things they refer back to:

> 'Otherwise, **he** relies on booze **you** could strip paint with.'
> 'Did **you** find **whoever** did **it**?'
> 'Find **them**?' Culley laughed. '**It** wasn't exactly a mystery. Stan wasn't eager to give evidence. **We** used a wages robbery for a couple of **them** some time later. **I** don't think **it** was **theirs**, but **it** served its purpose.
> 'Do **you** enjoy your job?' Kelso was turning his glass and tilting **it**, to shift the ice.
> 'Well,' Culley said, '**it** beats going to the office.'

The biggest problem writers have when using pronouns is making sure that it is clear to what or to whom particular pronouns refer.

To sum up, a pronoun can be the subject, object, or COMPLEMENT of a clause:

SUBJECT	VERB	OBJECT
I	love	you.
SUBJECT	VERB	COMPLEMENT
It	was	you!

Noun phrases

A word or group of words that forms a CLAUSE ELEMENT (e.g. the SUBJECT) is called a PHRASE. Phrases are examined in detail in Chapter 8.

We have seen that a noun can be the subject, object or complement of a CLAUSE. But nouns don't often stand on their own in this way. More frequently they form the HEADWORD of a NOUN PHRASE. Noun phrases are made up of four elements:

DETERMINER + PREMODIFIER + HEADWORD + POSTMODIFIER

Determiners

While it is true that you can use the single noun *elephants* as the subject, you cannot use *elephant*. *Elephant eats grass* is not a complete clause; it needs something else. For example:

SUBJECT	VERB	OBJECT
An *elephant*	*eats*	*grass.*

There is more about determiners on page 67.

The commonest type of word to come before a noun in this way is the article: *a / an / the.*

There are several other words that serve a similar purpose:

> *this, that,* etc.
> *my, his, her,* etc.
> *some, any,* etc.

All these words help to give the noun slightly greater definition, and are called determiners.

Modifiers

Modifiers before the noun

Our noun headword *elephant* can be given a lot more definition by adding words before it to MODIFY its meaning:

SUBJECT			VERB	OBJECT
A	*hungry young bull*	*elephant*	*eats*	*grass.*
DETERMINER	MODIFIERS	HEADWORD		

There is more about adjectives later in this chapter and also on pages 50–52.

Hungry and *young* are both ADJECTIVES modifying *elephant*. One way of building up a noun phrase is just to string a number of adjectives together before the noun:

DETERMINER	MODIFIERS	HEADWORD
a	*large purple*	*house*
a	*fast and powerful*	*car*

It is not only adjectives that can come before a noun to modify it. In the phrase *a hungry young bull elephant, bull* also modifies the noun. It tells us the elephant is a male. But *bull* is a noun, and nouns are frequently used before a noun headword to modify it.

Modifiers after the noun

We can also give information to define the noun by placing words after it. For example:

MODIFIERS in a
NOUN PHRASE
are examined in
more detail on
pages 72–74.

SUBJECT			VERB	OBJECT
That	*elephant*	*behind the tree*	*is eating*	*grass.*
DETERMINER	HEADWORD	MODIFIER		

So the headword of a noun phrase can be both PREMODIFIED and POSTMODIFIED:

DETERMINER	PREMODIFIERS	HEADWORD	POSTMODIFIERS
this	*appealing*	*property*	*on Silver Lane*
a	*modern semi-detached*	*property*	*that offers good-sized accommodation*

Adjectives

For more about
adjectives, see
also pages 50–52.

We have seen one very important feature of adjectives: they are placed before a noun to modify it. Most adjectives can be used in this way, which is called ATTRIBUTIVE.

But adjectives can also be used in another way: as a complement. We can use an adjective as a subject complement. For example:

SUBJECT	VERB	COMPLEMENT
Elephants	*are*	*big.*

This use of adjectives is called PREDICATIVE. Most adjectives can be used both attributively and predicatively, but a few are restricted to one or other of the two categories. For example *alone* can only be used predicatively. We can't talk about *an alone person*.

Types of adjective

An important way of categorising adjectives is into QUALITATIVE and CLASSIFYING adjectives. Qualitative adjectives give information about the qualities of the noun they modify. Examples are *big, hungry,* and *expensive.* Classifying adjectives place the noun into a class or category such as *pregnant, annual,* and *western.*

Qualitative adjectives

The categorising of adjectives might seem interesting but unimportant, except for the fact that qualitative adjectives can be graded. By putting certain words in front of them and GRADING them we can comment on how much of the quality the noun has.

Compare these three phrases:

an intelligent student

a highly intelligent student

a fairly intelligent student

The use of *highly* and *fairly* makes an *extremely* big difference to the meaning.

Qualitative adjectives can also be COMPARATIVE or SUPERLATIVE:

ABSOLUTE	*big*	*beautiful*
COMPARATIVE	*bigger*	*more beautiful*
SUPERLATIVE	*biggest*	*most beautiful*

Single syllable adjectives and certain two-syllable adjectives add *-er* and *-est.* Most adjectives of two syllables and almost all of three or more syllables use *more* and *most.*

Classifying adjectives

Classifying adjectives cannot be graded. For example it would be odd to describe a school prize-giving as *a highly annual event.* Even so, sometimes people break this 'rule' to achieve a special effect, for example: *She was looking very pregnant.* The word people make most fuss about is *unique.* Since this adjective means 'the only one of its type', they object that it is impossible to have something that is **very** unique. On the other hand, there is nothing wrong with saying that something is **almost** unique.

Other examples of classifying adjectives are:

agricultural	*chemical*	*daily*	*female*
golden	*magic*	*private*	*standard*

Ordering

As we have seen, it is possible to put a string of adjectives in front of a noun to modify it. English is quite fussy about the order in which the adjectives are placed. We learn this as we learn the language and most native speakers would have no difficulty in recognising that the adjective order in this phrase is wrong:

a wooden grey large house

The general order is:

1. qualitative adjectives
2. colour adjectives
3. classifying adjectives.

So it should be:

a large grey wooden house

What is this thing called 'verb'?

In Chapter 2, we saw that every sentence has to contain a verb. In this chapter we take a closer look at verbs and related grammatical features.

The word 'verb'

Rather confusingly, the word 'verb' is used in two different ways:

❑ to describe a WORD CLASS

❑ to describe a CLAUSE ELEMENT

Verbs as a word class

In this sense, verbs are on the same level as nouns, adjectives and ADVERBS.

Verbs as words are described in more detail in Chapter 7.

One of the key features of verbs is that they change their form, or INFLECT more than other words.

Verb inflection

Verbs inflect like this:

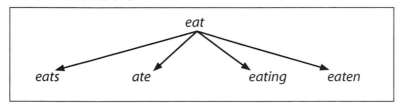

eat → eats, ate, eating, eaten

Forms of the verb

So we can say that all verbs have five forms, or parts:

❑ STEM   *walk*

❑ PRESENT TENSE *walk/walks*

❑ PAST TENSE   *walked*

❑   *-ing* PARTICIPLE   *walking*

❑   *-ed* PARTICIPLE   *walked*

We can can use the STEM to form the INFINITIVE: *to walk.*

Regular and irregular verbs

All verbs do not work in the same way as the example we have used. *Walk* is regular. Irregular verbs are less predictable in the way they form the five parts:

❑   STEM   *eat*

❑   PRESENT TENSE   *eat/eats*

❑   PAST TENSE   *ate*

❑   *-ing* PARTICIPLE   *eating*

❑   *-ed* PARTICIPLE   *eaten*

There are far more regular verbs than there are irregular, but many of the commonest verbs are irregular:

STEM	PRESENT TENSE	PAST TENSE	*-ing* PARTICIPLE	*-ed* PARTICIPLE
be	*am is are*	*was were*	*being*	*been*
go	*go goes*	*went*	*going*	*gone*
swim	*swim swims*	*swam*	*swimming*	*swum*
swing	*swing swings*	*swung*	*swinging*	*swung*
hit	*hit hits*	*hit*	*hitting*	*hit*

Main verbs

We saw in Chapter 2 that verbs could be divided into three groups:

❑   verbs that need an object
    *Elephants **eat** grass.*

❑   verbs that do not need an object
    *Elephants **exist**.*

❑   linking verbs
    *Elephants **are** animals.*

Verbs that need an object

In normal speech, *Elephants eat…* is incomplete because it leaves us asking, *eat **what?*** Verbs like *eat* that need an object are called TRANSITIVE.

Verbs that do not need an object

Exist on the other hand does not have to be followed by an object and is an INTRANSITIVE verb.

It is important to note that some verbs can be both transitive and intransitive. For example, *work*:

> *It's a formula that is obviously **working**.*

> *He trains people to **work** the machine.*

Linking verbs

These verbs are used to link a subject and its complement. They include *be, seem,* and *appear.*

Every sentence must contain at least one MAIN VERB. Another name for main verbs is LEXICAL verbs. That is because they are verbs with a meaning that you can look up in a dictionary.

Auxiliary verbs

There is also a group of verbs that don't have a dictionary meaning, and are not normally used on their own in a sentence. They are used with main verbs. For example:

A

> *I **am** eating bread.*

> *They **have** eaten bread.*

> *You **do** eat bread.*

B

> *I **shall** eat bread.*

> *I **might** eat bread.*

> *I **could** eat bread.*

All these verbs are called AUXILIARIES because they *help* main verbs. They have been divided into groups A and B, because they have different characteristics.

Primary verbs

The verbs in Group A, *be*, *have*, *do* can also work as main verbs. For example:

> I **am** *happy to see these names included.*

> I **have** *a new life now and new friends.*

> *We* **do** *things that are controversial.*

These primary verbs are thus dual-function.

Modal auxiliaries

The verbs in Group B cannot work as main verbs and normally appear with a main verb. The full list is:

> *will*   *shall*   *would*   *should*
> *may*   *might*
> *can*   *could*
> *must*
> *ought (to)*

There is a big difference between the meanings of the two sets of auxiliaries. The sentence that follows illustrates this:

> *It must work dependably.*

If you change this to *It works dependably*, you are saying something very different. We can use the contrast between the two types of auxiliary to make a point, as in this example:

> *Britain's labour market* **may be working** *better but it* **is** *still not* **working** *well.*

Here the comparative *better* is contrasted with the absolute *well*, and the MODAL AUXILIARY **may** *be working* is contrasted with the PRIMARY AUXILIARY **is** *working*.

To sum up: modal auxiliaries create a range of **possible** situations from *may* through *will* to *must*. The primary auxiliaries deal in **actual** situations.

Verbs as a clause element

In this sense verbs are on the same level as subjects, objects, complements, and adverbials. To be more accurate they should be described as VERB PHRASES.

In Chapter 2 when we looked at the different parts of a clause, the main examples contained verb phrases that consisted of just one word. This restricted us to just two tenses, the PRESENT TENSE and the PAST TENSE. Some linguists only use the term TENSE in this way, to describe two contrasting forms of the verb: *eat/eats* and *ate*. On this basis they say that English has no future tense. Newcomers to modern grammar find this somewhat disconcerting. What about *I will eat* – isn't that the future tense of *eat*? And if it isn't the future tense, what is it?

A more pragmatic way of looking at things is to use the term 'tense' in a looser and wider way: to describe the form of the verb phrase that provides information about time and aspect. That is how the term will be used in this book.

In tenses, *time* refers to past, present, and future; ASPECT refers to the focus that the verb phrase gives us on what is being described.

> Verb phrases are described in more detail in Chapter 8.

English tenses

The list of English tenses in this table will be familiar to modern language teachers:

	PAST	PRESENT	FUTURE
SIMPLE	she lived	she lives	she will live
CONTINUOUS	she was living	she is living	she will be living
PERFECT	she had lived	she has lived	she will have lived
PERFECT CONTINUOUS	she had been living	she has been living	she will have been living

Tense and aspect

We have already seen one form of the present tense:

Elephants eat grass.

English has, however, more than one form of the present tense. Compare these two sentences:

> I **eat** plenty of vegetables and I don't like chocolate.

> The ladies watching the late afternoon episode of 'Cross-roads' **are eating** Mr Kipling cakes from their local Safeway, wearing their Crimplene trouser suits.

They are both 'present' in the sense that both describe something that is true at the time of writing. But only the second describes something that is obviously happening at that moment. We call the first (*eat*) the SIMPLE PRESENT, and the second (*are eating*) the PRESENT CONTINUOUS.

There is also a third form of the present. Compare this sentence with the two previous ones:

> I **have eaten** there; it is wonderful and not ferociously expensive.

It refers to an event that happened in the past, but the speaker is still thinking about it – its effects, good or bad, are still in his or her mind. So, it is in one sense 'present'. In another sense it is past, completed – the action has been 'perfected'. Hence the name of this tense, the PRESENT PERFECT.

These three versions of the present tense, simple, continuous and perfect are called ASPECTS. They allow us to use considerable sophistication when talking about events.

Tense and time

Despite the wide range of tenses English has to offer, there are also many other ways in which we can indicate time in our sentences. The simple present tense, for example, can be used to talk about past, present, future and timeless events:

> He **goes** into a restaurant and he **says,** 'Oh the waiter, erm, let me see the menu...' (past)

> Rooney **shoots**... It's a goal! (present)

> Tomorrow we **enter** the mountains, and everything will change. (future)

> Fairly pure water **freezes** at about 0°C (if given sufficient time). (timeless)

Future time, in particular, is represented in a variety of ways:

> Tomorrow we **enter** the mountains, and everything will change.
> (Simple present used for scheduled actions.)

> Next year we **are** also **developing** a school-wide Booster Club.
> (Present continuous used for plans.)

> Yes, we **are going to change** the world of the media!
> (*going to* future for plans.)

> We **shall look** at these issues more fully later on.
> (*will/shall* future: unmarked future)

It is important to note that in many cases the precise time of an event is shown by a combination of verb phrase and one or more words which indicate time (*Thursday, next week* and so on.) These adverbials form an important part of the next chapter.

Active and passive

So the verb phrase provides a lot of information about time (through the tense) and about the speaker's perspective (through the aspect). Transitive verbs offer one further variation: VOICE. The following two sentences convey the same information, but they do so in different ways:

See also pages 79–80.

1. *Herb Gardner wrote the screenplay.*
2. *The screenplay was written by Herb Gardner.*

The focus of sentence 1 is on *Herb Gardner*; the focus of sentence 2 is on the screenplay and *Herb Gardner* becomes the agent, the means by which the screenplay got written:

	SUBJECT	VERB	OBJECT
ACTIVE	*Herb Gardner*	*wrote*	*the screenplay.*
PASSIVE	*The screenplay*	*was written*	*by Herb Gardner.*
	SUBJECT	VERB	AGENT

Sentences that follow the pattern, subject + verb + object can usually be transformed in a similar way.

The ACTIVE VOICE is by far the more common. The PASSIVE VOICE is restricted to certain specialised types of text (for example, scientific or academic) and to situations where the active would require a long-winded or awkward expression, as in the following sentence:

Several trucks were damaged by their sumps hitting rocks.

The passive is also a convenient way of avoiding responsibility for your own actions (…*and then the window got broken…*)!

Adverbs and other awkward customers

So far we have looked at basic clause patterns, noun phrases, verb phrases, and a number of word classes. Now we are left with something of a 'job lot' of phrases and word classes to consider.

Adverbs and adverbials

First we must distinguish between adverbs and adverbials:

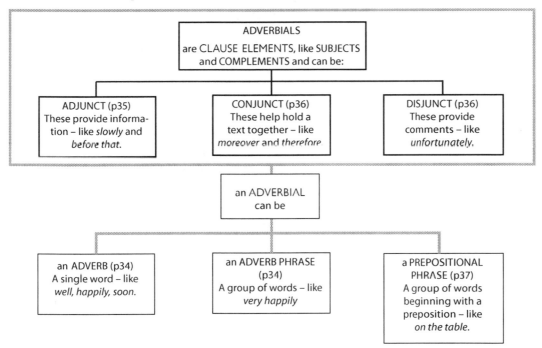

- ❏ An adverb is a single word and adverbs are a WORD CLASS like nouns and adjectives.

- ❏ An adverbial is a clause element like subjects and objects.

- ❏ An adverbial may be an ADVERB or it may be something else, as we shall see.

❑   An adverb can also form part of an ADVERB PHRASE or an ADJECTIVE PHRASE.

The diagram on the previous page shows how this works – and how this chapter sets out to explain them.

Adverbs

There is more about ADVERBS on pages 60–61.

To begin with, forget the one about 'adverbs end with -*ly*'. A lot of very important adverbs don't (for example, *tomorrow*, *here*, and *fast*). And there are words ending in -*ly* that aren't adverbs, like *friendly* and *silly*.

Adverbs are a class of words that can:

1. act as an adverbial:
    *The anger came **later**.*

2. form the headword of an adverb phrase:
    ***luckily** for us*

3. be used to modify an adjective in an adjective phrase:
    ***very** stupid*

4. be used to modify an adverb in an adverb phrase:
    ***rather** rashly*

5. be formed from many qualitative adjectives by the addition of -*ly:*
    *slow–**slowly***

Intensifiers

There is more about PHRASES in Chapter 8.

There is more about INTENSI-FIERS on page 60.

Numbers 2, 3, and 4 above show how adverbs can be used in the formation of phrases. Adverbs used to alter the meanings of adjectives and other adverbs are known as INTENSIFIERS. They can make them stronger:

*I think it's **incredibly** dangerous.*

or weaker:

*It was **slightly** fuzzy.*

or sit on the fence:

*He sounds **quite** interesting.*

Whatever effect we achieve, these adverbs are called intensifiers. It is possible to pile them up one on top of another, too:

> Our trade union structure is **quite extraordinarily** intricate…

If you use adverbs to intensify adjectives as in the examples above, you are creating adjective phrases. So, for example, *slightly sick* is an adjective phrase. If you intensify adverbs in a similar way, you create an adverb phrase. For example:

> This happened **very quickly**.

Here the intensifier *very* modifies the adverb *quickly* to create an adverb phrase *very quickly*.

Adverbials

Adverbials can be divided into ADJUNCTS, CONJUNCTS and DISJUNCTS. Of these, the first is by far the largest group.

There is more about ADVERBIALS on pages 92–94.

Adjuncts

The bulk of these provide answers to the questions, 'When?' 'Where?' and 'How?'

When?

Adverbials can provide information about:

- the point in time at which something happens
  *Fears that takeover talks at Morgan Crucible have hit a snag sent investors rushing for the exit **yesterday**.*

- how long it goes on for
  *I can't be a tourist **forever**.*

- how frequently it occurs
  *He **rarely** ate red meat.*

Where?

These adverbials tell us about:

- position
  *'It's glorious **here**,' he said.*

- direction
  Years ago someone told me that if you played Led Zeppelin's

*Stairway to Heaven song **backwards** that you could make out "satanic messages".*

How?

This is a much larger group of adverbials which tell us about the manner in which something occurred:

*Louise watched him **fastidiously**.*

Sentence focus

There is a small, but important, group of adverbials that add to the meaning of the sentence in a different way, by focusing attention on a part of it. For example:

*The Pope, **too**, has spoken warmly of unity.*

***Only** France has the mystique of the grandes écoles.*

In the first of these examples, the adverb *too* makes it clear that *The Pope* is being added to the list of those who have spoken warmly of unity. In the second, *only* has the opposite effect: it separates *France* from all other countries.

> CONJUNCTS and ADJUNCTS are two of the ways in which we give a text cohesion. This kind of analysis is not dealt with in this book – although we hope to publish in the future a separate title on the grammar of writing.

Sentence adverbials: conjuncts and disjuncts

There are two other groups of adverbs that we use to help stick a text together (or, linguistically speaking, 'give it cohesion'). For example, in the middle of an argument you might come across a sentence that begins with the word *Therefore*:

*Compromise, in general, is a crucial aspect to a President's success in working with Congress. The President's political party very rarely also controls Congress. **Therefore**, the President must work with Senators and Representatives who disagree with his agenda.*

Therefore is a conjunct. It links the present sentence with what has gone before. Other conjuncts are *however*, *moreover* and *similarly*.

A disjunct, on the other hand, makes a comment on part of the text, as *Fortunately* does in this text:

*There are some seriously talented and experienced individuals online and **fortunately** they are very helpful as well.*

Other disjuncts are *admittedly*, *probably*, and *clearly*.

Prepositional phrases as adverbials

Pretty much all the functions of adverbs that have been described so far can also be done by groups of words that are not themselves adverbs. Compare these pairs of sentences:

*Let me know **tomorrow**.*
*Let me know **at the end of the week**.*

*You want to hang it **there**.*
*You want to hang it **above the fireplace**.*

*Fat Watt watched them go **smugly**.*
*Fat Watt watched them go **with a satisfied air**.*

In each case the adverb has been substituted by a phrase of similar meaning. Each of these is a PREPOSITIONAL PHRASE, so called because it begins with a PREPOSITION. Most prepositional phrases begin with a preposition, followed by one of the following:

❑   a NOUN
   *for **elephants***

❑   a PRONOUN
   *for **them***

❑   a NOUN PHRASE
   *for **the bulk of the population***

Prepositions

These small words or word groups get their name because they are positioned before ('pre') a word or group of words. They can consist of one word (*up, down, in,* etc.) or two (*out of, close to,* etc.) or more (*as well as, in the course of,* etc.).

Other uses of prepositional phrases

For the sake of completeness, it's worth pointing out that prepositional phrases don't only work as adverbials. They also often form part of other phrases.

In noun phrases

They are often used as modifiers in noun phrases, as in these examples:

*...a teacher **from one of the local primary schools**...*

Some people call groups of words that function as ADVERBIALS in a CLAUSE 'adverbial phrases'. This can be confusing. It is better to name phrases after their HEADWORD (NOUN PHRASE, ADJECTIVE PHRASE etc). Using this system an ADVERB PHRASE is a phrase with an adverb as its headword – like *very slowly,* while an ADVERBIAL is an element in a

Where this wins over the dance floor bandwagon jumpers is in its **upfront and in your face** *approach rather than being docile.*

In adjective and adverb phrases

They can also occur in adjective and adverb phrases, particularly those involving comparison:

Normally the most charismatic species go extinct first -- the most colorful birds, the biggest **of the mammals***, the most exciting* **of the insects and amphibian***s...*

As a subject complement

They can come after verbs like *be* to provide more information about the subject. For example:

Dirty bomb alert was **over the top***, White House admits.*

To sum up

The ways in which prepositional phrases can be used are summed up in this diagram:

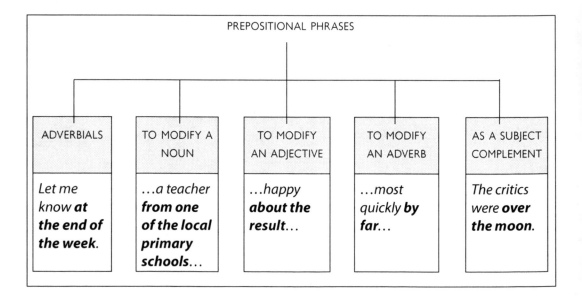

PREPOSITIONAL PHRASES				
ADVERBIALS	TO MODIFY A NOUN	TO MODIFY AN ADJECTIVE	TO MODIFY AN ADVERB	AS A SUBJECT COMPLEMENT
Let me know **at the end of the week***.	*...a teacher* **from one of the local primary schools***...	*...happy* **about the result***...	*...most quickly* **by far***...	*The critics were* **over the moon***.

Real-life sentences

So far we have only dealt with short simple sentences: the analysis in Chapter 2 was based on sentences of no more than four words. In this chapter we'll apply the ideas introduced so far to longer sentences.

Three types of sentence

We can divide sentences into three broad groups according to the number of clauses they contain and how these are linked.

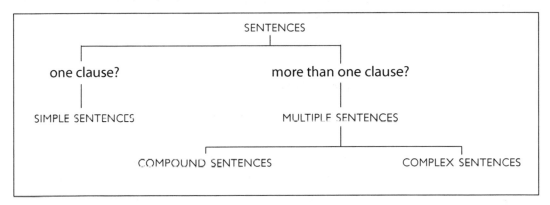

Simple sentences

A sentence that consists of just one clause is described as a simple sentence. This does not tell us anything about its length or about the ideas it contains. Both the following examples are simple sentences on the pattern SUBJECT + VERB + OBJECT:

> *Elephants like grass.*

> *The dynamic world of flamenco takes a contemporary twist.*

The second sentence seems much more complicated than the first, but it isn't really. It starts with a noun phrase:

> *The dynamic world of flamenco*

This is based on the headword *world*. The object of the sentence is also a noun phrase based on the headword *twist*.

We shall re-visit sentences in Chapter 10.

So grammatically the sentence boils down to:

SUBJECT	VERB	OBJECT
world	*takes*	*twist*

Compound sentences

The simplest way of joining two clauses is to use *and* or *but*. For example:

> *I told him **and** he shook his head in admiration*

> *Travelling was a slow, tedious business **but** the difficulties were not insuperable.*

And and *but* are CONJUNCTIONS (a term deriving from the Latin for joining two things together). The two items they join are of equal status in the sentence, so they are described as CO-ORDINATING CONJUNCTIONS. Other similar conjunctions are *or, then, yet*.

Co-ordinating conjunctions can also be used to join words and phrases. For example:

> *bread **and** butter*

> *the budget **or** the general election.*

Complex sentences

When clauses are linked in a different way we create something called a COMPLEX SENTENCE. The term 'complex' describes the grammatical structure and not the length of the sentence or its complexity of meaning.

In a complex sentence, one clause is grammatically superior to the others. This clause is the MAIN CLAUSE and any other clauses are SUBORDINATE to it. The best way to show how this works is to take a simple sentence and then turn it into a complex one.

SUBJECT	VERB	COMPLEMENT
Her message	*was*	*short and to the point.*

SUBJECT	VERB	COMPLEMENT
What she told us	*was*	*short and to the point.*

Here we started with a subject that was a noun phrase and have substituted a clause for it, so that we end up with two clauses. Although a complex sentence has a main clause, this does not mean that the main clause is necessarily one that will stand alone if you pull it out of the sentence:

SUBORDINATE CLAUSE	MAIN CLAUSE
What she told us	*was short and to the point.*

Nominal clauses
A clause that does the job of a noun phrase as subject, object or complement is a NOMINAL CLAUSE. (Nominal clauses are sometimes referred to as NOUN CLAUSES.)

Relative clauses
Noun phrases may contain a clause that modifies the headword. Such clauses are called RELATIVE CLAUSES and are introduced by the relative pronouns *who(m)*, *which* and *that*. Again the clause can replace a single word or a phrase:

*Gordon Beamish was a **lynx-eyed** man.*
(ADJECTIVE)

*Gordon Beamish was a man **with eyes like a lynx**.*
 (PREPOSITIONAL PHRASE)

*Gordon Beamish was a man **who made a fetish out of being lynx-eyed**.*
(RELATIVE CLAUSE)

Relative clauses can also be introduced by a ZERO RELATIVE pronoun – that is to say, no relative pronoun at all:

*The book **you lent me** is really interesting.*

Adverbial clauses
Adverbial clauses can be regarded in the same way.
For example:

*So I went round **later**.* (ADVERB)

*So I went round **after work**.* (PREPOSITIONAL PHRASE)

*So I went round **after I had finished**.* (ADVERBIAL CLAUSE)

Adverbial clauses can do most of the things that single adverbs, or phrases (especially prepositional phrases) used as adverbials can. The main functions of adverbial clauses are detailed in Chapter 10.

To end this section, here is a short piece of text with the adverbial clauses printed in bold.

> **When I was well again** it became clear that Tsiganok occupied a very special place in the household. Grandfather didn't shout at him so often and so angrily **as he did at his sons**, and **when he wasn't there** he would screw up his eyes, shake his head, and say, 'My Ivanka's got hands of gold.'

You will notice that a common feature of adverbial clauses is that they are introduced by words like *when, as, if, because*. Since they introduce subordinate clauses, these are referred to as SUBORDINATING CONJUNCTIONS.

A bit more about verbs

Verbs are described in much more detail in Chapters 7 and 8.

All the clauses we have looked at so far have contained a FINITE VERB.

The word 'finite' is linked to 'finished' and means that the verb in question is complete. Compare these two simple sentences:

> An old woman **walking** on the side of the road with two goats traipsing beside her. ✗

> An old woman **was walking** on the side of the road with two goats traipsing beside her. ✔

The first 'sentence' is not a complete sentence. It might do as the caption for a photograph, or as part of a set of informal notes. It doesn't, however, provide the kind of complete information that a full sentence does. It prompts the question, *What about the old woman walking from the Doon Bridge into Alloway village?*

Grammatically, it is incomplete because it does not contain a finite verb. The finite parts of the verb are the present and past tense forms. A finite verb therefore is either in the past tense, or – if in the present – it changes according to the subject in NUMBER and PERSON. The *-ing* participle (for example, *walking*) and the *-ed* participle (for example, *eaten*) cannot stand alone as a finite verb.

Where there is more than one verb in the verb phrase, it is the first verb that has to be finite. For example:

> He **was** being told...

> They **have** been making...

Non-finite clauses

A clause that contains a finite verb is described as a finite clause. It is possible to have NON-FINITE CLAUSES. These work in a similar way to finite clauses but contain a non-finite verb. For example:

> **Walking** back to the hotel, Rozanov and I were silent for a long time.

The non-finite clause *Walking back to the hotel* could be transformed into: *As we were walking back to the hotel*. It is an ADVERBIAL CLAUSE giving information about time. Other examples and transformations are:

> **Taken piece by piece** the face was lovely.
> **When you took it piece by piece** the face was lovely.

> The aim is **to sell the product at markets**.
> The aim is **that we should sell the product at markets**.

Verbless clauses

It is also possible to have a clause that has no verb at all. You can usually spot these because they are introduced by a SUBORDINATING CONJUNCTION. For example:

> **Although not unattractive**, he was cut in a rougher mould than his father.

Here the clause could be transformed into a finite clause:

> **Although he was not unattractive**, he was cut in a rougher mould than his father.

Similar verbless clauses and transformations are:

> These are now on order and will be circulated **when available**.
> These are now on order and will be circulated **when they become available**.

Although under fire from enemy positions on three sides, Lieutenant Calhoun effectively directed his boats in suppressing the enemy fire...

Although Lieutenant Calhoun was under fire from enemy positions on three sides*, he effectively directed his boats in suppressing the enemy fire...*

PART B

The details

In this chapter each class of words is treated separately: nouns, adjectives, verbs, adverbs, pronouns, prepositions, determiners, and conjunctions.

Word classes

> In traditional grammar, word classes were called 'parts of speech'.

Words can be divided into classes according to the way in which they are are used. The eight main word classes can be represented in a diagram like this:

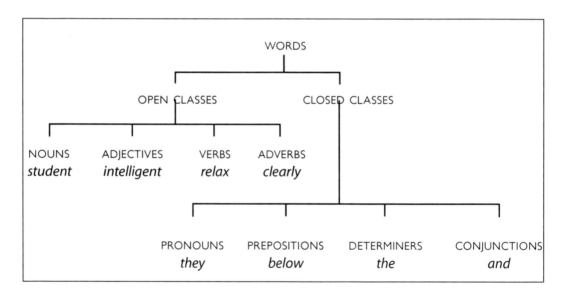

So why divide words into 'open' and 'closed' classes?

Open classes

These are described as 'open' because they are still having new words added to them. For example a search of the internet site Word Spy at the time of writing found *gurgitator, antigriddle, e-thrombosis,* and *fratire*. (The site is well worth a visit: go to www.wordspy.com)

Words in these open classes are sometimes also called 'content' words, because they have a lexical content: they are words you can look up in a dictionary and find a meaning for.

Closed classes

These classes are not having new words added to them, so they are closed. If you look them up in a dictionary you will not find a definition so much as an explanation of how they are used. They are sometimes referred to as 'structure words', because they are used to build the structure of sentences.

Nouns

Nouns satisfy all or most of these criteria:

❑   They can be SINGULAR or PLURAL:
one bunch; two bunches

❑   They can stand as the headword of a noun phrase:
a bunch of carrots

❑   They can be modified by an adjective:
a large bunch

> The part played by nouns in building sentences is explored in Chapter 3.

The majority of nouns refer to people, places, things, and ideas.

Categories of nouns

Nouns fall into a range of categories, the most useful of which can be summed up in this simple diagram:

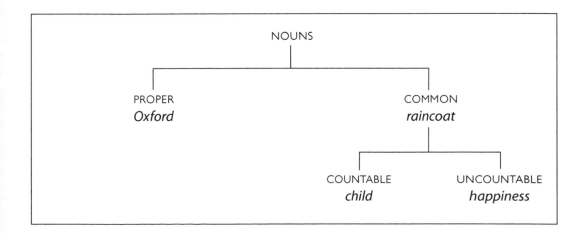

Proper nouns

Proper nouns refer to people, places, things and ideas that are unique. They are often written with initial capital letters and include:

Some writers no longer use capital letters in this way, but the convention is still widespread.

❑ The names of individual people and places
Jane, Paris

❑ The names of organisations, institutions, publications, films, TV programmes, pieces of music and other things that are unique
Congress, Hamlet

❑ People's titles when used to refer to an individual, with or without their personal name:
the Professor, the President
This does not apply when the title is used generically:
some professors
the five presidents of Central America

Common nouns

All nouns except for proper nouns fall into this group. Common nouns can be countable or uncountable.

Countable and uncountable nouns

Most common nouns have singular and plural forms, because they refer to things that can, in theory at least, be counted. Most English nouns make their plural form by adding -s or -es, and some, like those for words ending in -f, have slightly more complex plural forms. A very small number either have a completely irregular plural form, like *child, mouse* and *woman*, or have the same form for both singular and plural – like *sheep*.

Uncountable nouns

A relatively small number of common nouns are not normally used in the plural because they are regarded as uncountable. Examples of these are:

anger	*behaviour*	*butter*	*childhood*	*courage*	*earth*
electricity	*existence*	*flesh*	*fun*	*growth*	*happiness*
health	*help*	*loneliness*	*luck*	*magic*	*milk*
mud	*music*	*pride*	*rain*	*salt*	*sand*

Clearly many, but not all, of these are abstract nouns (*butter* and *milk*, are exceptions). Some can be used in the plural in special circumstances:

> *Lurpak, the cream of Danish **butters**, brings a taste of Europe to your table…*

Since proper nouns refer to people, places, things and ideas that are unique, they are by definition uncountable.

The distinction between countable and uncountable nouns is important when we decide which determiners to use before them. The diagram that follows shows the most important of these.

There is more about determiners later in this chapter, on page 67.

WORDS	COUNTABLES		UNCOUNTABLES	EXAMPLE
	SINGULAR	PLURAL		
little, less, least	✗	✗	✔	less hassle
few, fewer	✗	✔	✗	fewer delays
much	✗	✗	✔	much excitement
many, several	✗	✔	✗	many surprises
these	✗	✔	✗	these episodes

In other words:

> *fewer trains* ✔
> *less trains* ✗

Adjectives

Main uses

Attributive

Adjectives help to narrow the meaning of nouns, by giving further information. They are normally used before the noun, which they are said to modify:

> It also has a **new** president.

Although adjectives normally come before the noun, they can also come after it:

> Chen telephones Nicaragua to congratulate President **elect** Ortega.

Placing an adjective against a noun to modify it is called the ATTRIBUTIVE use of adjectives.

Predicative

Adjectives can also be used after verbs such as *to be* in sentences like this:

> One thing is **certain**.

This use is described as PREDICATIVE (since the adjectives form a key part of the PREDICATE of the sentence).

The verb to *be* is a LINKING VERB. there is more about these verbs on pages 27 and 55.

Limitations

A small number of adjectives can only be used attributively. For example:

> adoring   belated   fateful   paltry   scant   thankless

Some adjectives are almost always used predicatively. For example:

> afraid   alive   alone   asleep   glad   ill
> likely   ready   sorry   sure   unable   well

Types of adjective

Most adjectives can be allocated to one of two large groups:

```
                        ADJECTIVES
        ┌───────────────────┴───────────────────┐
   QUALITATIVE                              CLASSIFYING
      dull                                    annual
```

Qualitative adjectives

These refer to a quality that can be attributed to someone or something. For example:

anxious   *fresh*   *simple*   *young*

Classifying adjectives

By contrast, these adjectives allocate things and people to a particular group or class. For example:

annual   *British*   *urban*   *southern*

Grading

Qualitative adjectives can be graded – that is to say you can have more or less of the quality they refer to:

This is a topic that some who visit the elderly find **extremely boring***, just as others find it fascinating.*

The usual way of grading adjectives is by placing an intensifying adverb before the adjective. Common adverbs for this purpose are:

amazingly	*awfully*	*deeply*	*dreadfully*
exceedingly	*extremely*	*heavily*	*highly*
horribly	*incredibly*	*remarkably*	*really*
strikingly	*terribly*	*very*	

Classifying adjectives are not normally graded in this way. For example it would not make much sense to say:

It became an **extremely annual** *event…*   ✗

There are, however, circumstances in which we make such adjectives gradable to achieve a special effect:

Kangaroo Poo Paperweights: **more Australian** *than a shrimp on the barbie - buy one today!*

Comparison

We can also compare things using adjectives:

But she's right about one thing: we do need a **bigger** *house.*

Lanzarote is possibly the **most unusual** *island in the world.*

Adjectives thus have three forms:

ABSOLUTE	COMPARATIVE	SUPERLATIVE
big	*bigger*	*biggest*
unusual	*more unusual*	*most unusual*

Formation

This occasionally causes problems. The rules are these:

1. Words of one syllable form the comparative and superlative by adding *-er* and *-est* respectively.

2. Two-syllable adjectives ending in *-y* also add *-er* and *-est* (although the *'y'* normally changes to an *'i'*: *happy–happier*).

3. Most of the remaining two-syllable adjectives and all three-syllable adjectives use *more* and *most* to form the comparative and superlative.

4. There is a small group of two-syllable words which can follow either rule. These include:

    common   cruel   narrow   pleasant
    remote   shallow   simple   stupid

5. There is also a small group of three-syllable words that can follow either rule. They are negative forms of the words in Rule 2 with the PREFIX *un-* added to them and include:

    uneasy   unhappy   unlikely   unlucky   unsteady

Verbs

It is important to remember that the term verb is used in two ways:

❏   to refer to a word class (as noun and adjective are). In this sense verbs are always single words

❏   to refer to a clause element (as subject and object are). In this sense we should more accurately refer to the verb phrase, which may consist of a single word or may include up to five words, all of which will be verbs in the first sense.

The verb phrase is described in detail in the next chapter, on pages 76–81. Clause elements are dealt with in Chapter 9.

In this chapter we are looking at verbs as a word class. We can classify verbs in this way:

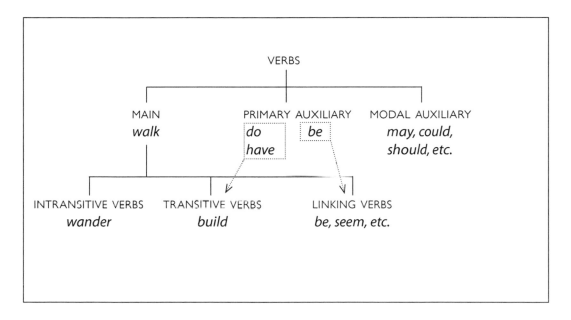

Main verbs

These are also called 'full', or 'lexical' verbs because they are verbs which contain meaning – you can look them up in a dictionary and find a definition. They can appear on their own as the verb in a sentence:

*My head **aches**.*

*The fishermen **shook** their heads.*

Types of main verb

Most main verbs can be allocated to one or more of these three groups:

- ❑ TRANSITIVE verbs

- ❑ INTRANSITIVE verbs

- ❑ LINKING verbs

Transitive verbs

The OBJECT of a clause is explained on pages 10–11 and 89.

These are verbs that take an object:

SUBJECT	VERB	OBJECT
We	will take	turns.

Certain transitive verbs are followed by two different types of object:

SUBJECT	VERB	INDIRECT OBJECT	DIRECT OBJECT
He	bought	me	a brandy.
You	have granted	him	the desire of his heart.

In such sentences, the direct object refers to the thing that is directly acted upon by the verb and the indirect object refers to the person or things that benefit from the action. Clauses of this type can be transformed like this:

SUBJECT	VERB	INDIRECT OBJECT	DIRECT OBJECT
He	bought	me	a brandy.

SUBJECT	VERB	DIRECT OBJECT	INDIRECT OBJECT
He	bought	a brandy	for me.

Verbs of this type are sometimes referred to as DITRANSITIVE verbs. Common ditransitive verbs are:

bring	find	get	give	hand
leave	lend	make	pass	sell
send	show	take	teach	tell

Intransitive verbs

These are verbs that do not take an OBJECT:

Mr Gobind Patel and his wife Nanbai **escaped**.

Most explicit price-fixing **has gone**.

Typical intransitive verbs are:

arrive	die	disappear	happen	laugh
relent	rise	speak	vanish	work

Linking verbs

These are verbs which link a SUBJECT and its COMPLEMENT:

I **am** *the son of a king. It suddenly* **appeared** *rather middle-class.*

Common linking verbs are:

appear	be	become	feel	get
look	seem	smell	sound	taste

The SUBJECT COMPLEMENT of a clause is explained on pages 12–13 and 90.

Some verbs can fall into more than one of the three groups.

Transitive and intransitive

A number of verbs can be used with or without an object:

Candice is **eating** *a dish of beans and preserved goose.*
(transitive)

She was always **eating**.
(intransitive)

Other verbs that can be either transitive or intransitive are:

change	drive	fit	hold	hurt
meet	miss	run	study	win

Linking and intransitive

Some verbs that are used as linking verbs can also function as intransitive verbs.

*However, conflicting findings have **appeared**.*
(intransitive)

*He said he was all right but **appeared** very shocked.*
(linking)

Other verbs of this type are:

   go   grow   remain   stay   turn

Auxiliary verbs

As their name suggests, these 'help' the main verb within the sentence, by extending its functions. In these examples, the verb phrase is in bold type and the auxiliary verbs are boxed:

I |*have been*| *watching a film.*

At the end of March I |*will have*| *completed six years.*

Then he |*could*| *leave early, and get on with the business.*

Auxiliary verbs form two groups:

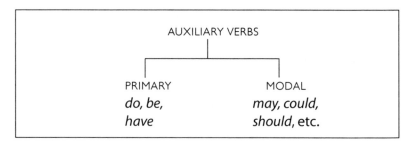

Primary auxiliaries

The primary auxiliaries are: *be, have, do.*

Examples of these are:

Detectives |*are*| *working on the theory that the bags had been there for some time.*

I |*have*| *bought   a house in Herededas.*

But you |*do*| *not sound bothered.*

These three verbs can also occur on their own as MAIN VERBS:

*They **are** very audible.*

*The House **has** accommodation for 272 residents in a combination of one, two and three bedded rooms.*

*He **did** a quick sum.*

Modal auxiliaries

The modal auxiliaries are:

will	*shall*	*would*	*should*
may	*might*		
can	*could*		
must			
ought (to)			

These verbs are used to build verb phrases which refer to possible events rather than actual events. Compare the following pairs of sentences:

*Ask him if he thinks I **have visited** Mr Conchis.*
*Ask him if he thinks I **might visit** Mr Conchis.*

*They **have not reassured** the public.*
*They **will not reassure** the public.*

Inflection

Verbs inflect; that is to say that they change their form according to the subject and the sentence in which they are used. They do this in two ways.

Tense

Many modern grammarians use the word 'tense' in a very restricted way. They use it to mean the way in which the form of the verb is changed to give information about time. In this sense, English only has two tenses: present and past.

PRESENT	PAST
she walks	*she walked*
he sings	*he sang*

Most English verbs are regular and make the past tense by adding *-ed* to the stem of the verb.

The word 'tense' is also used in a broader way. This is explained in detail on pages 77–79.

Number and person

The form of the verb depends on the subject. As the following table shows, regular verbs have one form for *he, she,* and *it* and another for the other persons. The verb *be* is even more varied.

		PRONOUN	VERB: *walk*	VERB: *be*
SINGULAR	1ST PERSON	*I*	*walk*	*am*
	2ND PERSON	*you*	*walk*	*are*
	3RD PERSON	*he/she/it*	*walks*	*is*
PLURAL	1ST PERSON	*we*	*walk*	*are*
	2ND PERSON	*you*	*walk*	*are*
	3RD PERSON	*they*	*walk*	*are*

The subject and the verb have to agree (and you will sometimes see agreement referred to as CONCORD). Failure to make subject and verb agree is a common mistake in writing.

Forms of the verb

Verbs appear in a number of different forms:

STEM / INFINITIVE	*walk*
PRESENT PARTICIPLE	*walking*
PAST PARTICIPLE	*walked*
PRESENT TENSE	*walk(s)*
PAST TENSE	*walked*

Irregular verbs

However, some of the commonest verbs in English do not follow this pattern and have irregular forms for the past tense and the PAST PARTICIPLE. There are about 250 of these irregular verbs. These are some examples:

STEM	PAST TENSE	PAST PARTICIPLE
begin	*began*	*begun*
bite	*bit*	*bitten*

STEM	PAST TENSE	PAST PARTICIPLE
break	*broke*	*broken*
forbid	*forbade*	*forbidden*
go	*went*	*gone*
hit	*hit*	*hit*
read	*read*	*read*
swim	*swam*	*swum*
swing	*swung*	*swung*
write	*wrote*	*written*

Adverbs

The main uses of adverbs can be summed up as follows:-

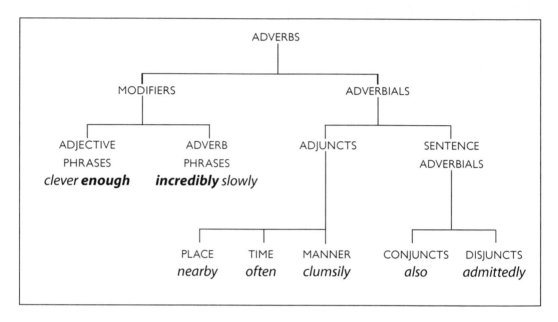

Modifiers

Adverbs can form part of adjective phrases and adverb phrases.

Adjective phrases

There is more about adjective phrases on pages 83–84.

An adjective phrase has an adjective as its headword and can be modified by an adverb. This usually comes before the adverb:

*This seems **highly** unlikely.*

Adverb modifiers can also come after the adjective headword:

*I'm just clever **enough**, and no more.*

Adverbs commonly used in this way (as intensifiers) are:

amazingly	*awfully*	*deeply*	*dreadfully*
exceedingly	*extremely*	*heavily*	*highly*
horribly	*incredibly*	*remarkably*	*really*
strikingly	*terribly*	*very*	

Adverb phrases

Adverbs can be used to modify other adverbs in a similar way to that used with adjectives:

> He moved **incredibly** slowly.

> But it works well **enough**.

There is more about adverb phrases on page 85.

Adverbials

Adverbs can also appear as adverbials in a sentence. They can be used as one of the following:

❑ ADJUNCTS
These 'add' meaning to the clause or sentence in which they are used.

❑ CONJUNCTS and DISJUNCTS (SENTENCE ADVERBIALS)
These contribute to the coherence of the text in which they are used.

Adjuncts

When adverbs are used as adjuncts, they can provide information about place, time, and manner.

Adjuncts are explored in more detail on pages 93–94.

Place

Adverbs can add information about position:

> There are mountains **nearby**.

They can also give information about direction:

> I scuttled **backwards** and hid behind the curtains.

Adverbs commonly used in these ways are:

above	here	nearby
there	below	backwards

Time

Adverbs answer these questions:

❑ When?
*We'll do that **later**.*

❑ For how long?
*We met **briefly** at the Pitts' party.*

❑   How frequently?
    *These clubs **often** run tours and other events to take part in.*

Other examples of time adverbs are:

WHEN?	FOR HOW LONG?	HOW FREQUENTLY?
afterwards	*always*	*continually*
finally	*briefly*	*never*
later	*indefinitely*	*occasionally*
soon	*overnight*	*often*
suddenly	*permanently*	*seldom*
then	*temporarily*	*sometimes*

Manner

Adverbs of manner describe *how* an action is performed:

*He imagined her waiting **pathetically** by the phone.*

Like *pathetically*, most adverbs of manner are formed from adjectives by adding the SUFFIX -*ly*:

awkwardly   beautifully   cleverly   clumsily
doubtfully   gloomily   slowly   tipsily

Sentence adverbials

Adverbials are also used to give a text cohesion, to glue the different parts of it together. They can help link one sentence to another (conjuncts) and they can be used to make a comment on what is being said (disjuncts). Adverbials of this type may be a group of words, or a single word. Single word conjuncts and disjuncts are normally adverbs.

Conjuncts

Adverbs commonly used in this way are:

also   besides   finally   first(ly)   however
next   otherwise   similarly then   therefore

For example:

*Today is at leisure in Knysna. This quaint seaside village is
full of arty-crafty shops and roadside curio stalls to browse*

*through. **Alternatively**, you might like to delve into the past and catch the historic Outeniqua Choo-Tjoe steam train to George and back.*

Disjuncts

Adverbs commonly used in this way are:

admittedly	*clearly*	*fortunately*	*frankly*
generally	*incredibly*	*personally*	*possibly*

For example:

*What sort of exercise? **Frankly**, provided you follow a few basic rules…it really doesn't matter.*

> Sentence adverbials are sometimes called CONNECTIVES.

Pronouns

It is often said that pronouns 'stand in for nouns'. While that is true, they also 'stand in for' a number of other grammatical forms. The following labelled paragraph illustrates some of them:

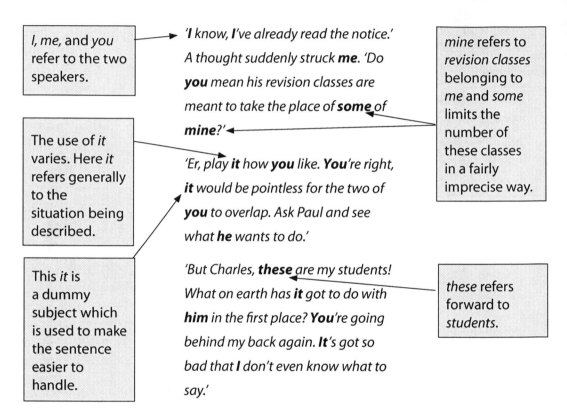

I, me, and *you* refer to the two speakers.

'I know, I've already read the notice.' A thought suddenly struck me. 'Do you mean his revision classes are meant to take the place of some of mine?'

mine refers to *revision classes* belonging to *me* and *some* limits the number of these classes in a fairly imprecise way.

The use of *it* varies. Here *it* refers generally to the situation being described.

'Er, play it how you like. You're right, it would be pointless for the two of you to overlap. Ask Paul and see what he wants to do.'

This *it* is a dummy subject which is used to make the sentence easier to handle.

'But Charles, these are my students! What on earth has it got to do with him in the first place? You're going behind my back again. It's got so bad that I don't even know what to say.'

these refers forward to *students.*

Different types of pronoun

There is a wide range of pronouns available:

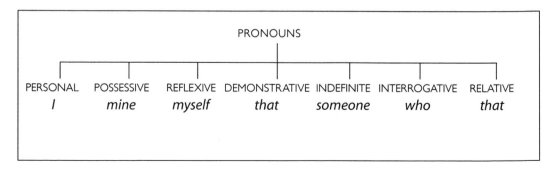

			PRONOUNS			
PERSONAL	POSSESSIVE	REFLEXIVE	DEMONSTRATIVE	INDEFINITE	INTERROGATIVE	RELATIVE
I	*mine*	*myself*	*that*	*someone*	*who*	*that*

Personal pronouns

These refer to people, places, things, and ideas:

	SINGULAR		PLURAL	
	SUBJECT	OBJECT	SUBJECT	OBJECT
1ST PERSON	*I*	*me*	*we*	*us*
2ND PERSON	*you*	*you*	*you*	*you*
3RD PERSON	*she/he/it*	*her/him/it*	*they*	*them*

As the table shows, personal pronouns have two CASES: one refers to the subject (*I, she* etc.) and the other to the object (*me, her* etc.) The objective case is also used after pronouns.

Possessives

There are two types of possessive:

❑ POSSESSIVE DETERMINERS, which come before a noun
   *The doctors must be called to explain **their** differences.*

❑ POSSESSIVE PRONOUNS, which stand on their own
   *But shareholders own the firm: the decision should be **theirs**.*

POSSESSIVE DETERMINERS	POSSESSIVE PRONOUNS
my	*mine*
your	*yours*
his/her/its	*his/hers/its*
our	*ours*
your	*yours*
their	*theirs*

Reflexive pronouns

	SINGULAR	PLURAL
1ST PERSON	*myself*	*ourselves*
2ND PERSON	*yourself*	*yourselves*
3RD PERSON	*herself/himself/itself*	*themselves*

Reflexive pronouns allow us to refer back to the subject later in the sentence:

> She bought **herself** an entire wardrobe of new clothes.

> I eat the leftovers **myself**.

Demonstrative pronouns

> this   that   these   those

These help us refer to people or things in terms of space or within a text or dialogue:

> Often **this** has proved to be so.

> **Those** were the years when Romania carried off the prizes.

Indefinite pronouns

> someone   somebody   something
> anyone   anybody   anything

These are used when you don't want to, or cannot be more precise about the person or thing you are referring to:

> **Nobody** is more capitalist than the amateur athlete.

> We are under no pressure to do **anything** immediately.

Interrogative pronouns

> who   whom   which   what

These are used for asking questions:

> **Whom** did Gavrilo Princip shoot in June 1914?

They are also used for making exclamations

> **What** a full, rich life you lead!

Relative pronouns

> who   whom   which   that

These are used to introduce relative clauses:

> They will have specialists with **whom** they like to work.

> Richie stooped to pluck a wild oat **that** had strayed into the wood.

Determiners

Some nouns can stand on their own in a sentence:

Happiness *is no laughing matter.* (UNCOUNTABLE NOUN)

I understand she told **John** *the same story before she promised to marry him...* (PROPER NOUN)

Baboons *will gang up on a leopard in a similar way, although this is a risky venture.* (PLURAL NOUN)

Many, however, will not. For example, you cannot begin a sentence, *Baboon will not...* Most of the time nouns are preceded by one or more determiners. This is a list of the most common:

1	2	3
all, both	a, an, the	two, three, etc.
half, two-thirds, etc.	this, that, these, those	third, seventh, etc.
such	my, our, your, his, her, its	other, last, next
	some, any, no	many, few, little, much

Of these, by far the commonest are the articles *a(n)* and *the*. As these examples show, it is possible to have more than one determiner before the noun:

Mutual suspicion killed **this** *agreement.*

Half my *clients don't even want to let me know what they're up to.*

Someone is in the middle and **all the other** *children in the circle are holding hands.*

When there is more than one determiner the order in which they appear is that of the columns in the chart above.

Certain determiners are restricted in their use. Numerals, for example cannot be used with uncountable nouns. While we can use *much/more/most* with both countable and uncountable nouns, the same is not true of *little/less/least*. These words should only be used with uncountables. With countables the words are *few/fewer/fewest*. So it's *less sand* but *fewer grains of sand*.

> Types of NOUN are described on pages 47–49. NOUN PHRASES are explained on pages 72–75.

> There is more about COUNT-ABLE and UNCOUNTABLE

Prepositions

Prepositions are a small(ish) class of words, many of which refer to position in space and time. As their name suggests they are placed (-*position*) before (*pre-*) something else. They can come before:

❑ a NOUN
   beyond *hope*

❑ a PRONOUN
   after *you*

❑ an ADJECTIVE (used as a noun)
   in *blue*

❑ a NOUN PHRASE
   after *his last performance*

❑ a CLAUSE
   after *what you have just said*

Common prepositions

The commonest prepositions are:

about	*after*	*as*	*at*	*before*
between	*by*	*during*	*for*	*from*
in	*into*	*of*	*on*	*over*
than	*through*	*to*	*under*	*with*
within	*without*			

There are also prepositions which consist of more than one word:

❑ two-word prepositions
   according to ; out of

❑ three-word prepositions
   in line with ; on top of

❑ four-word prepositions
   by the side of; in the course of

Conjunctions

We use conjunctions to join together two grammatical elements. A conjunction like *and* can join:

❑ WORDS
*Then **you** and **I** would both be sorry.*

❑ PHRASES
*But he denied possessing **the vegetable** and **the iron bar** as imitation firearms.*

❑ CLAUSES
The door swung back slowly, silently,** and **he went in.

Conjunctions can be of two kinds:

❑ CO-ORDINATING

❑ SUBORDINATING

Co-ordinating conjunctions

These join together two items that are of equal grammatical status. In the examples above, the sentence grammar gives no indication as to which of the two things joined by *and* is more important. The commonest co-ordinating conjunctions are:

and	*but*	*nor*
or	*then*	*yet*

See also the section on COMPOUND SENTENCES on page 99.

Subordinating conjunctions

These make it clear that one item is subordinate to the other. Among the commonest are:

after	*although*	*as*	*because*	*before*
if	*since*	*so (that)*	*though*	*unless*
until	*when*	*where*	*wherever*	*while*

See also the section on COMPLEX SENTENCES on pages 100–104.

Like co-ordinating conjunctions, subordinating conjunctions can introduce:

❑ WORDS
*Chief Executive George Mathewson received an appropriate **if unusual** memento.*

❑ PHRASES
*A charming **if somewhat absent-minded** companion.*

❏   CLAUSES
*It would be in everyone's interests **if the plans were quietly
dropped.***

Phrases

A phrase is a group of words that works as a single unit within a clause. The three commonest types of phrase are noun phrases, verb phrases and prepositional phrases.

Types of phrase

Words can be joined together to form larger grammatical elements called phrases. For example see how the meaning of the following sentence develops as we build up a noun phrase on the word *collector*:

Jonathan Gili was	*a* collector.
Jonathan Gili was	a **discriminating** collector.
Jonathan Gili was	a **highly** discriminating collector.
Jonathan Gili was	a highly discriminating collector **of sardine tins**.
Jonathan Gili was	a highly discriminating collector of sardine tins **and Star Wars figures**.
Jonathan Gili was	a highly discriminating collector of sardine tins, **fridge magnets**, and Star Wars figures.

Each type of phrase is named after the class of word upon which it is based – its headword:

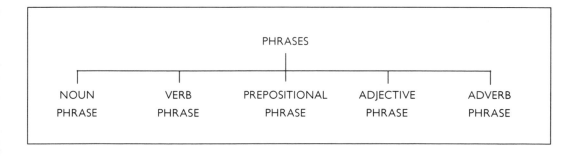

Noun phrases

A noun phrase is built up on a single noun headword.

Structure of the noun phrase

The headword can have words on either side of it, like this:

DETERMINERS	PREMODIFIERS	HEADWORD	POSTMODIFIERS
a	highly discriminating	collector	of sardine tins, fridge magnets, and star Wars figures

Determiners

There is a more detailed description of DETERMINERS on page 67.

Although nouns can stand on their own in a sentence, they often need the support of at least one other word, as can be seen from this non-sentence:

News is bad.

It is grammatically incomplete. The noun subject needs to be preceded by a word such as *the* or *this*. These, and words like them, make the reference of the noun more precise. This can be seen from these three sentences:

The *people should be given the vote.*

Some *people should be given the vote.*

My *people should be given the vote.*

Each has a different meaning because of the word that precedes the noun. Words in this group are called determiners. The commonest are the ARTICLES:

a   an   the

Modifiers

Adding one or more determiners is the first step in the construction of a noun phrase. The second is to add or alter the meaning of the noun, by modifying it. We can do this by placing words before, or after, the headword: this is known as premodification and postmodification.

Premodifiers

ADJECTIVES are the commonest type of premodifier. For example:

> a **smooth** politician

> a **leading German** politician

It is not just adjectives that can be used like this. Nouns can function in a similar way:

> a **journalist** politician

and so can parts of verbs:

> a **disgraced** politician

You can even use a noun phrase within a noun phrase:

> a prominent **left wing** politician

Postmodifiers

It is also possible to add words after the noun to modify it. This is most commonly done using a prepositional phrase:

> a politician **of great experience**

Relative clauses

The other main way in which a noun can be postmodified is by using a clause:

> the politician **who promised 'peace in our time'.**

Up to now we have been working on this principle:

```
SENTENCES

are made up of

CLAUSES

which are
made up of

PHRASES

which are
made up of

WORDS
```

So it comes as a bit of a surprise to find that phrases can contain clauses. Fortunately relative clauses are an exception, rather than a regular pattern, and they can be very useful.

Structure

Relative clauses are introduced by one of the following:

RELATIVE PRONOUN	RELATIVE DETERMINER	RELATIVE ADVERB	ZERO RELATIVE
who	whose	where	Sometimes a relative clause is introduced by nothing at all.
whom		when	
which		why	
that			

Examples

*There were many **who wanted Alexander dead.***
(*who* as CLAUSE SUBJECT)

*She had also decided to invite Louise and Miriam, **whom she wanted to impress with her domestic abilities.***
(*whom* as CLAUSE OBJECT)

*And was it mostly the bigger farms **that wanted you**?*
(*that* as CLAUSE SUBJECT)

*Is that the point **that you wanted to make**?*
(*that* as CLAUSE OBJECT)

*You may even be a member of a non charitable student society **which wants to run a charity event**.*
(*which* as CLAUSE SUBJECT)

*It was an event **which no one wanted to miss**.*
(*which* as CLAUSE OBJECT)

*It was the main reason **why the marriage was never to take place**.*
(*why* as CLAUSE ADVERBIAL)

*Midlife is a time **when the results of bad posture can cause trouble**.*
(*when* as CLAUSE ADVERBIAL)

*Faliraki is a lively town **where you'll find a host of tavernas, bars, and discos**.*
(*where* as CLAUSE ADVERBIAL)

*The last thing **they wanted** was unexpected demands for cash from ITN.*
(ZERO RELATIVE as CLAUSE OBJECT)

Uses of noun phrases
Noun phrases can form part of:

❑ a CLAUSE

❑ a PHRASE

Within a clause
A noun phrase can form any of the following parts of a clause:

❑ SUBJECT
Botswana's semi-arid climate *limits the range of crops.*

❑ DIRECT OBJECT
*It was almost as if he'd hit **some kind of a block.***

❑ INDIRECT OBJECT
*He told **the court** that he had been under 'emotional stress' at the time of the offence.*

❑ SUBJECT COMPLEMENT
*Pat is **my older sister.***

❑ OBJECT COMPLEMENT
*It was this certainty that made her **the leader.***

❑ ADVERBIAL
*All three of those had just arrived **the day before.***

Within a phrase
A noun phrase can form part of a phrase in a variety of ways. The commonest of these are:

❑ PREPOSITIONAL PHRASE
*In **other ways** , Katherine's life was less pleasurable.*

❑ NOUN PHRASE
*She got a **first class** degree at the end of it all.*

Verb phrases

VERBS as a
WORD CLASS are
described in detail
on pages 25–28.

The grammatical term 'verb' can have two somewhat different meanings: a WORD CLASS (like NOUN) and a CLAUSE ELEMENT (like SUBJECT). The verb in a clause is sometimes one word, a verb:

> My head **aches**.

> Then the retired postman **pulled** the trigger.

Often, however, the verb in a clause consists of more than one word. For example:

> Someone **must have been watching** us.

> His heart **will have started to race** as he looked left and right and saw the two main practice strips.

Whether the verb in a clause is one word or several, it is more correctly referred to as the verb phrase. Verb phrases can combine main and auxiliary verbs to convey a wide range of meanings.

Structure of the verb phrase

The verb phrase can consist of up to four words, all of which must be verbs:

My head	*aches.*			
	MAIN			
Richard	*is*	*reading*	*a letter.*	
	PRIMARY	MAIN		
It	*has*	*been*	*working*	*miracles.*
	PRIMARY	PRIMARY	MAIN	
Without us, it	*might*	*work.*		
	MODAL	MAIN		
Cynics	*might*	*have*	*said*	*we were too folksy.*
	MODAL	PRIMARY	MAIN	
It looked as though we	*might*	*have*	*been*	*cooking*	*the books.*
	MODAL	PRIMARY	PRIMARY	MAIN	

Strictly speaking the verb phrase can consist of five verbs, but only in the passive (see pages 31–32) and only very rarely in expressions such as

> By now she **should have been being seen** by the doctor.

But examples are rare in real usage – and that one was invented.

English tenses

Some grammarians define a tense as an INFLECTION of the verb – a change of meaning you achieve by altering the form of the verb. So the past tense of *win* is *won*. In this sense, English only has two tenses, present and past. But for everyday use – especially for those who are studying foreign languages – this strict definition of tense is not very helpful. There is a broader use of the word, which is what will be used here: a form of the verb phrase which gives information about aspect and time. Using the word in its broader sense, English has the following 'tenses':

	PRESENT	PAST	FUTURE
SIMPLE	I see	I saw	I shall/will see
CONTINUOUS	I am seeing	I was seeing	I shall be seeing
PERFECT	I have seen	I had seen	I shall have seen
PERFECT CONTINUOUS	I have been seeing	I had been seeing	I shall have been seeing

It is this wide variety that makes English tenses so difficult for foreign learners. Whereas French, for example, has only one present tense, *je vois*, English has two, *I see* and *I am seeing*. When you add in the vast range of possibilities opened up by modal auxiliaries other than *shall* and *will*, the scope for sophistication – and confusion – becomes immense:

> I **may have been being** a bit selfish.

The main uses of each tense are described in the Glossary under the relevant headings.

Aspect

The aspect of the verb phrase gives us information about the nature of the action or state referred to. There are three aspects in English: CONTINUOUS, PERFECT, and SIMPLE.

Continuous aspect

This is also called the progressive aspect:

> Richard **is reading** a letter.

It is commonly used to focus on the continuous nature of an action: the fact that it went on over a period of time. The present continuous is also used to refer to the future when something is planned:

> The award **is being presented** tomorrow.

Perfect aspect

This aspect is generally used to describe actions that have been completed, but the effects of which are, or were, still present or relevant in some way at the time referred to:

> Anyone who **has read** 'Smallholder' over the last few years will know I love the Autumn.
> (PRESENT PERFECT)

> After he **had read** it aloud he crumpled the note up in his fist and thrust it into the fire.
> (PAST PERFECT)

Simple aspect

This contrasts with the other two aspects. They focus attention on a particular feature of the verb phrase in relation to time. The simple aspect is general. In the present tense it is used for habitual actions:

> At bedtime he **reads** me stories.

and general truths:

> Pure water **freezes** only at 0°C, and boils at 100°C.

Tense and time

The form of the verb phrase is not the only way in which we give information about time. Indeed, English can be rather cavalier about the way in which it applies its tenses. We use the context of the rest of the sentence to supplement or even subvert the tense of the verb. The simple present, for example, can be used to refer to the past:

*Two mathematicians **are** in a bar. The first one **says** to the second that the average person **knows** very little about basic mathematics. The second one **disagrees**. The first mathematician **goes** off to the washroom, and in his absence the second **calls** over the waitress. He **tells** her that in a few minutes…*

It can also refer to the future:

*We **fly** from here to Nanking on April 17th, and from Nanking to Shanghai, we **go** by train on May 8th.*

Finite verbs

English speakers sometimes have problems in making sure that a sentence contains a finite verb. A finite verb shows tense. If it is in the present tense it also shows number and person. (This also applies to the past tense of the verb *be*.) A simple sentence must contain a finite verb if it is to be grammatically complete. If there is only one word in the verb phrase, then that must be finite:

*Miss Punkney **went** scarlet.* ✔

*Miss Punkney **gone** scarlet.* ✘

If there is more than one word in the verb phrase, then the first word must be finite:

*Lately Chihaya **has been having** some disturbing nightmares.* ✔

*Lately Chihaya **been having** some disturbing nightmares.* ✘

Active and passive

Transitive verbs are verbs that can be followed by an object:

SUBJECT	VERB	OBJECT
Lightning	*has struck*	*the tree.*

In clauses that follow this pattern:

❏ the subject (*Lightning*) refers to the actor

❏ the verb (*has struck*) refers to some kind of action

❏ the object (*the tree*) refers to something that is acted upon.

It is possible to turn clauses like this round so that we see the events from the point of view of the object:

There is more about transitive verbs on pages 54–55.

SUBJECT	VERB	AGENT
The tree	*has been struck*	*by lightning.*

The verb changes from the active voice to the passive voice:

has struck ⟶ *has been struck*

The passive is formed using the primary auxiliary *be* plus the past participle.

The great advantage of the passive is that you don't have to have an agent at all; you can construct sentences on the pattern:

Some basic rules were broken.

Glue was squirted into Mr K's locks, and windows were broken.

In each case the speaker may know who was responsible, but isn't obliged to say. The active is much more common than the passive, which tends to be reserved for special situations such as formal English and scientific reports.

The subjunctive

This is a form of the verb (technically a MOOD) used for a small number of situations.

Present subjunctive

This takes the form of the stem of the verb and is used in three main ways:

❑   to express wishes
    *After appearing before a magistrate, Vanunu was released on bail on condition that he **remain** under 'house arrest' at the cathedral for the next seven days.*
    *The king is dead, long **live** the king.*

❑   to make suppositions
    *I can't tell you how many times I've walked off stage to see producers sitting there in tears, whether it **be** happiness or frustration.*

❑   to give instructions
    *They insisted that she **consult** a psychiatrist and, fortunately, Laura had the strength to insist that it **be** a woman.*

Past subjunctive

This only applies to one word: *were*. It is used to refer to hypothetical situations that are either impossible:

> *I'd be careful if I **were** you, Rose.*

or fairly unlikely:

> *And when she hung up, he kept the phone to his ear as if
> she **were listening** still.*

Prepositional phrases

PREPOSITIONS are described on page 68.

A prepositional phrase is a phrase that begins with a preposition headword.

Structure

The preposition headword is usually followed by:

❑   a NOUN
    He left just a few days before ***Christmas...***

❑   a PRONOUN
    Jinny squatted beside ***him.***

❑   certain ADJECTIVES
    Selene was in ***green**; but Paul did not notice what Selene wore.*

❑   a NOUN PHRASE
    This uneasy halfway house is fair game for ***the worst excesses of journalism.***

❑   a NON-FINITE CLAUSE containing A PRESENT PARTICIPLE
    Peter planned to beat the rush by ***leaving at the end of May.***

❑   a CLAUSE beginning with *who, which, how,* etc.
    Many pilots select the days on ***which they fly** so that the weather is near ideal and not too windy.*

Use

The main ways in which prepositional phrases can be used are:

ADVERBIALS are described on pages 92–94.

NOUN PHRASES are described on pages 72–75.

ADJECTIVE and ADVERB PHRASES are described on pages 83–85.

❑   as the ADVERBIAL in a clause
    *You want to hang it **above the fireplace**.*

❑   as part of a NOUN PHRASE
    *The land **beside the pond** looks tired too...*

❑   as part of an ADJECTIVE or ADVERB PHRASE
    Victor Emmanuel of Savoy is not the brightest of fellows...

❑   as a SUBJECT COMPLEMENT
    *The critics were **over the moon**.*

Adjective phrases

A group of words built up on an adjective headword forms an adjective phrase.

Structure

Adjective phrases can be formed in three ways:

❑   by forming strings

❑   by PREMODIFICATION

❑   by POSTMODIFICATION

Strings

Adjectives are often used in strings of two or more:

>   a **large grey plastic** box

In strings like this each adjective helps narrow down what is being defined:

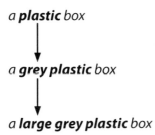

>   a **plastic** box
>
>   a **grey plastic** box
>
>   a **large grey plastic** box

Premodifiers

The commonest premodifiers are intensifying adverbs:

>   They are **extremely** heavy.

Postmodifiers

Adjectives can be postmodified by:

❑   an ADVERB
    *The statistics are impressive **enough**, but they hardly tell the story.*

❑   a PREPOSITIONAL PHRASE
    *He was still angry **about the coat**.*

❑   a NON-FINITE CLAUSE
    *They were happy **to be back**.*

> There is more about INTENSIFYING ADVERBS on pages 34–35 and 60–61.

❑   a FINITE CLAUSE
*You'll be so glad **that you did**.*
*Medical treatment for hay fever is now much better **than it** **used to be**.*

Adverb phrases

The formation of adjective phrases is described on pages 83–84.
Adverb phrases are formed in a similar way.

Strings

> All the time the train is carrying us **slowly but surely** up
> the French coast.

Premodifiers

> We must do that **fairly** soon.

> He signed a long-term contract **only recently**.

Postmodifiers

Adjectives can be postmodified by:

❑ an ADVERB
  *They usually found out fast **enough**.*

❑ a PREPOSITIONAL PHRASE
  *Adam Reed came on for the last half hour and did well **for a
  sixteen-year-old**.*

❑ a FINITE CLAUSE
  *Isabel shoved her chair back so quickly **that it almost top-
  pled over**.*

Clauses

Words and phrases are arranged into units called clauses. Clauses are made by combining five elements: subject, verb, object, complement, and adverbial.

Clauses are built up of five basic elements:

- ❑ SUBJECT
- ❑ VERB
- ❑ OBJECT
- ❑ COMPLEMENT
- ❑ ADVERBIAL

These elements can be combined to form seven basic clause patterns. These are listed, with examples, on page 95.

Subject

The subject is one of the two essential parts of a declarative clause. It often tells us what the sentence is about. To do this the subject has to refer to a person, a thing or an idea. In declarative clauses, it usually comes at or near the beginning of the clause and before the verb.

Structure

❑ Sometimes a single NOUN is enough to do this:
 Music *isn't my life any more.*

❑ At other times, the subject has already been defined and we can refer back to it, using a PRONOUN:
 Music isn't my life any more. *It* *takes up too much time.*

❑ Often we need to define the subject more precisely and so we build on a single noun or pronoun, creating a longer NOUN PHRASE:
 Early 18th century music *isn't my life any more.*

Othe possibilities are:

❑ an ADJECTIVE used as a noun:
 Green *is the most essential colour in the garden.*

❑ the *-ing* form of the verb used as a noun (the GERUND):
 Gardening *is a very satisfying hobby for many people.*

❑ the verb INFINITIVE:
 To err *is human…*

More detailed information:

NOUNS:
pages 47–49

PRONOUNS:
pages 64–66

NOUN PHRASES:
pages 72–75

ADJECTIVES:
pages 50–52.

Verb

The VERB PHRASE is described in more detail on pages 76–81.

The verb is the other essential part of a declarative clause, and it normally comes after the subject. It may be one word:

> I **spoke** to her politely.

Very often, however, the verb in a sentence consists of more than one word. For example:

> Lee **was being dragged** down the bank.

Whether the verb in a sentence is one word or several, it is more correctly referred to as the verb phrase.

Meanings and usage

Verbs can refer to:

❑ actions
> He **attacked** the door, which **caved in** at the third blow.

❑ states
> Creed **was sleeping** with his eyes wide open.

There is more about LINKING VERBS on page 55.

They are also used to link a subject with its complement:

> Later he **became** the vicar of a Cambridge parish.

Object

The object of a clause normally comes after the verb and refers to someone or something different from the subject:

*He ate **the food** and drank **the coffee**.*

The exception to this is when the object is a reflexive pronoun:

*She could hurt **herself**.*

The object often refers to someone or something that is affected by the action described by the verb, as in the examples above.

Verbs that take an object are called transitive verbs.

> You will find more about TRANSITIVE VERBS (and also about verbs that take two objects) on pages 54–55.

Structure

The object can be:

- ❏ a NOUN
  *They discussed **books** for a few minutes.*

- ❏ a PRONOUN
  *I have grown to dislike **it**.*

- ❏ a NOUN PHRASE
  *I forgot **the departmental meeting.***

- ❏ an ADJECTIVE used as a noun
  *No I don't like **red**…*

- ❏ the -*ing* form of the verb used as a noun (the GERUND)
  *If you enjoy **walking** you'll love the Forest.*

> More detailed information:
>
> NOUNS:
> pages 47–49
>
> PRONOUNS:
> pages 64–66
>
> NOUN PHRASES:
> pages 72–75
>
> ADJECTIVES:
> pages 50–52.

Complement

The word complement is used in grammar to refer to any grammatical feature which serves to complete another. In this book its use is confined to:

❑   the SUBJECT COMPLEMENT

❑   the OBJECT COMPLEMENT

Subject complement

The subject complement comes after the verb and provides more information about the subject. So the subject and the complement both refer to the same person or thing. Only a small group of verbs, linking verbs can be used for this purpose, and they act as a kind of linguistic equals sign:

> Anthony Evans is **a musician**.

> Anthony Evans = **a musician**.

By far the commonest linking verb is *be*. Others include *appear, become, feel, get, look, seem, smell, sound, taste*.

A complement can be any of the following:

More detailed
information:

NOUNS:
pages 47–49

PRONOUNS:
pages 64–66

NOUN PHRASES:
pages 72–75

ADJECTIVES:
pages 50–52

ADJECTIVE
PHRASES:
pages 83–84.

❑   a NOUN
*You and I are **teachers**.*

❑   a PRONOUN
*All I ever wanted was **you**.*

❑   a NOUN PHRASE
*Sportswear is **the new influence on high fashion**.*

❑   an ADJECTIVE
*He was **unhappy**.*

❑   an ADJECTIVE PHRASE
*On the other hand, his membership in the Austrian Academy of Sciences was **very important to him**.*

Object complement

This comes after the object and complements it in sentences like these:

> *Being a mother has made me **less selfish**.*

Among other things, we use clauses of this kind to refer to:

❑ giving someone a job
(for example *appoint, make, elect*)
*The newly established International Committee for Scientific Management (CIOS) appointed him **its first vice-president** in 1926.*

❑ expressing an opinion
(for example *consider, think, judge*)
*He considered it **more dangerous than any horse he had ever ridden**.*

❑ causing something to happen
(for example *drive, make, render*)
*The sound of her repeating a line back at him drove him **mad**.*

❑ keeping something in a particular state
(for example *keep, leave*)
*Maybe her love would have kept him **alive**.*

The object complement can be:

❑ a NOUN
*I didn't show my true colours until they made me **chairman**.*

❑ a NOUN PHRASE
*Local folk tales made it **the home of mythical monsters**.*

❑ an ADJECTIVE
*But psychology makes him **happy**.*

❑ an ADJECTIVE PHRASE
*It made her lazy, it made her **rather self-indulgent**.*

More detailed information:

NOUNS:
pages 47–49

NOUN PHRASES:
pages 72–75

ADJECTIVES:
pages 50–52

ADJECTIVE PHRASES:
pages 83–84.

Adverbial

There are a small number of transitive and intransitive verbs that require the clause to contain an adverbial:

> *Jessy lives **in a low income area of a town in Zambia.***
> (INTRANSITIVE)

> *Jackie put his head **on one side**.*
> (TRANSITIVE)

More frequently the adverbial is an optional clause element and can occur in a variety of places within the clause:

> *But **underneath the smiles and easy-going ways,** grim statistics linger.*

> *This is **partly** a consequence of simple arithmetic.*

> *He's **underneath the table**.*

Structure

The adverbial in a clause can be any one of the following:

❑ a single word, an ADVERB
*It would be peaceful **there**.*

❑ an ADVERB PHRASE
*It's all done **very quickly**.*

❑ a NOUN PHRASE
***The day before the war**, there was a demonstration.*

❑ a PREPOSITIONAL PHRASE
*I stood **in the rain**…*

More detailed
information:

ADVERBS:
pages 60–63

ADVERB PHRASES:
page 85

NOUN PHRASES:
pages 72–75

PREPOSITIONAL
PHRASES:
page 82.

Types

Like adverbs, adverbials fall into three broad groups:

❑ CONJUNCTS

❑ DISJUNCTS

❑ ADJUNCTS

Conjuncts are adverbials used to give a text cohesion by demonstrating the links between sentences.

*And he remembered Isaac's story about the man who thought too much and smiled once more. Not until dawn, **however**, could he fall asleep.*

Disjuncts are adverbials that can be used to make a comment on what is being said.

*   **Generally**, *the more snow, the less danger there is to skiers.*

*   *It was unfair to them, **quite frankly**.*

Adjuncts

Adjuncts 'add' to the meaning of the sentence in the following ways.

Place

Adverbials of place provide answers to questions like *Where? Whence?/From where?* and *Whither?/To where?* For example:

away	*down the road*
in Florida	*in the middle*
from the top of the hill	*there*

Time

Adverbials of time provide answers to the questions *When? For how long? How frequently?* For example:

at irregular intervals	*for several minutes*
now	*some time last week*
today	

Manner

These adverbials answer the question *How?* For example:

in a leisurely way	*with tears in her eyes*
quickly	

Purpose

These answer the question *Why?* For example:

*I cannot think of anyone who has sacrificed as much as he has on a personal level **in the cause of peace in this country**...*

> Some people call groups of words that function as ADVERBIALS in a CLAUSE 'adverbial phrases'. This can be confusing. It is better to name phrases after their HEAD-WORD (NOUN PHRASE, ADJEC-TIVE PHRASE etc). Using this system an ADVERB PHRASE is a phrase with an adverb as its headword – like *very slowly*, while an ADVERBIAL is an element in a clause.

Reason

These also answer the question *Why?* For example:

> *Appeals on their behalf have been suspended **because of the current situation in Iraq.***

Result

These refer to the effects of something happening:

> *But trains still racket by frequently **with ear-splitting effect**.*

Condition and concession

These speculate on the effects of one condition on another.

> ***If necessary**, we will support you through the court process.*

> *My friend thinks that the movie we saw last night was boring but I found it amusing **although rather ridiculous**.*

Clause patterns

These five clause components can be combined into a small number of basic clause patterns. The first four, subject, verb, object, and complement, can be combined to make five sentence or clause patterns in which all the components are compulsory: if you remove any of them the sentence becomes grammatically incomplete. They are:

SUBJECT	VERB
The war	has ended.

SUBJECT	VERB	OBJECT
I	forgot	the departmental meeting.

SUBJECT	VERB	INDIRECT OBJECT	DIRECT OBJECT
He	bought	me	a brandy

SUBJECT	VERB	SUBJECT COMPLEMENT
Anthony Evans	is	a musician.

SUBJECT	VERB	OBJECT	OBJECT COMPLEMENT
Psychology	makes	him	happy.

There are two patterns in which an adverbial is essential, but they are far less common:

SUBJECT	VERB	ADVERBIAL
Jessy	lives	in Zambia.

SUBJECT	VERB	OBJECT	ADVERBIAL
Jackie	put	his head	on one side.

More commonly, however, the adverbial is optional .

Language creativity

Although the patterns are simple, they form the basis of an infinite variety of clauses. For example:

SUBJECT	VERB	ADVERBIAL
Farming	*is*	*basic.*

can be developed into:

The substantial agricultural sector	*tends to amount to*	*little more than subsistence farming.*

Sentences

So how do we combine the seven different types of clause into sentences? This chapter examines the different types of sentence and how clauses are used within them.

Types of sentence

There are four types of sentence, as follows.

Declarative

These are sentences normally used to make statements like *Elephants are dangerous*. In declarative sentences the normal word order is to begin with the subject, followed immediately or fairly shortly afterwards by the verb.

Interrogative

These are normally used to ask questions. There are three types of interrogative question:

yes/no

These are question sentences that can normally only be properly answered by *yes* or *no*. For example:

> *Did you know that taramasalata is crammed with fat?*

wh- questions

These begin with a question word: *who/whom/whose, what, which, how, why, when, where*. They are open questions inviting a wide range of possible answers.

> *When did you last tell your partner that you find him or her very attractive?*

either/or

Some questions offer the respondent two possible answers. For example:

> *Does the benefit from education accrue to parents or children?*

Imperative

These are normally used to make commands, orders, requests and so on, for example:

> *Look at a particular point on the wall in front of you and try to relax.*

There is usually no sentence subject in such sentences, because *you* is understood.

Exclamative

These are used to make exclamations of various kinds. They begin with *What* or *How* and then place the object or the complement before the subject:

	SUBJECT	VERB	COMPLEMENT
	This country	*is*	*strange.*
How	*strange*	*this country*	*is!*
	COMPLEMENT	SUBJECT	VERB

Simple and multiple sentences

Sentences can be classified like this:

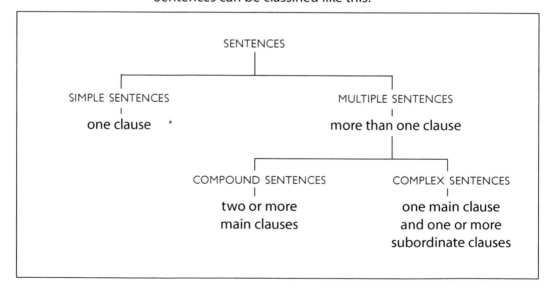

Simple sentences

Simple sentences consist of only one clause. They can be short:

Their farms are primitive.

or long:

The substantial agricultural sector tends to amount to little more than subsistence farming.

Compound sentences

If we restrict ourselves to simple sentences, it is difficult to express subtle shades of meaning. At its crudest, a succession of simple sentences can have a very childish ring to it:

We got up early. We went in the car. Maggie drove us to the seaside. It was a lovely day. The sun was shining...

So we need to combine clauses in a variety of ways.

At an early age children try to overcome this by stringing longer sentences together using conjunctions such as *and* and *then*. They have discovered the simplest way of constructing multiple sentences: building compound sentences.

In a compound sentence we simply bolt clauses together using co-ordinating conjunctions such as *and, but, then*. So these two clauses:

CO-ORDINATING CONJUNCTIONS are described in more detail on

I didn't go to work yesterday

my boss sacked me

can be combined in a variety of ways:

I didn't go to work yesterday, and *my boss sacked me.*

My boss sacked me, and *I didn't go to work yesterday.*

I didn't go to work yesterday, then *my boss sacked me.*

I didn't go to work yesterday, but *my boss sacked me.*

As you can see, these conjunctions do not throw much light on the relationship between the two clauses. *And* just joins them together, although the order in which we place the two clauses affects the meaning; *then* tells us that one occurred before the other; and *but* suggests that there is some kind of contrast or conflict between the two statements.

Complex sentences

If we want to express anything more sophisticated, we have to adjust the relationship between the two clauses. Instead of the two being of equal grammatical weight, one has to take over control of the sentence; it has to become the MAIN CLAUSE. The other clause(s) are then SUBORDINATE to it. In these versions of the sentence, the main clause is printed in bold type:

> **I didn't go to work yesterday** *because my boss sacked me.*

> **My boss sacked me** *because I didn't go to work yesterday.*

> **I didn't go to work yesterday**, *so my boss sacked me.*

> **My boss sacked me**, *so I didn't go to work yesterday.*

and so on.

If we keep the ideas and language but allow a little more freedom in the forms, we can develop many more possibilities of meaning:

> *If I hadn't gone to work yesterday,* **my boss would have sacked me**.

> **I didn't go to work yesterday** *so that my boss would sack me.*

Complex sentence patterns

Complex sentences follow similar patterns to simple sentences. The difference is that one or more of the components of the main clause becomes a subordinate clause rather than a phrase. So, for example, the subject, object, or complement can be a noun clause instead of a noun phrase:

MAIN CLAUSE		
SUBJECT	VERB	COMPLEMENT
His answer	was	a denial.
MAIN CLAUSE		SUBORDINATE CLAUSE
His answer	*was*	*that he just didn't know.*
SUBORDINATE CLAUSE	MAIN CLAUSE	SUBORDINATE CLAUSE
What he told us	*was*	*that he just didn't know.*

Each subordinate clause itself follows one of the basic patterns described in Chapter 9 (see page 95):

❑ SUBJECT + VERB

❑ SUBJECT + VERB + OBJECT

❑ SUBJECT + VERB + DIRECT OBJECT + INDIRECT OBJECT

❑ SUBJECT + VERB + SUBJECT COMPLEMENT

❑ SUBJECT + VERB + OBJECT + OBJECT COMPLEMENT

❑ SUBJECT + VERB + ADVERBIAL

❑ SUBJECT + VERB + OBJECT + ADVERBIAL

Functions of subordinate clauses

Subordinate clauses fulfil three main functions:

❑ they modify a noun or pronoun (RELATIVE CLAUSES);

❑ they do the jobs otherwise done by pronouns, nouns, or noun phrases (NOUN, OR NOMINAL, CLAUSES);

❑ they act as the adverbial in a clause or sentence (ADVERBIAL CLAUSES).

Relative clauses

Relative clauses form part of a noun phrase. They modify the headword, coming after it in the phrase:

NOUN PHRASE (AS SUBJECT)			REST OF SENTENCE
The	person	who comes to an interview smelling unfavourably	may be seen to be a 'bad' applicant.
DETERMINER	HEADWORD	RELATIVE CLAUSE	

Restrictive and non-restrictive relative clauses

Relative clauses are often an essential part of the sentence. In this sentence:

*...Is there one bus **that goes all the way in**?*

we cannot remove the relative clause without drastically changing the meaning of the sentence:

The structure and uses of RELATIVE CLAUSES are described on pages 73–75.

...Is there one bus?

Such relative clauses are described as RESTRICTIVE.

Sometimes, however, a relative clause is not essential to the meaning of a sentence and can be removed without loss of essential meaning:

*He also became a great favourite with the occupants of the local school bus, **which passed his garden gate twice daily**.*

Such NON-RESTRICTIVE relative clauses are normally:

❑ marked by commas or other punctuation

❑ introduced by *which, who* or *whom*.

Nominal clauses
A nominal clause can:

❑ be the subject, object, or complement of a clause:
   Whoever had done this *wished him harm.* (SUBJECT)

   *Both the New Yorker and the Washington Post have previously reported **that the Pentagon is studying military options on Iran.*** (OBJECT)

   *This is **what happened**.* (COMPLEMENT)

❑ form part of a prepositional phrase:
   *In 1988 the group had 8,000 employees, **of whom 500 were outside France**.*

❑ form part of a noun phrase:
   *A dominant factor is the idea **that Switzerland is expensive**.*

❑ form part of an adjective phrase:
   *She…was unhappy **that Ludovico had married**.*

Adverbial clauses

There is more information about ADJUNCTS on pages 93–94.

Adverbial clauses convey a range of important meanings. When used as adjuncts they can have these functions:

Space

*They went **where they liked**, played **where they chose**.*

Time

The cards and flowers arrived **when I got there**.

Reason

People climb mountains '**because they're there**'.

Purpose

The i2i system can also generate realistic background images **so that users can pretend they are somewhere else**.

Result

This virus affects the body's defence system **so that it cannot fight infection**.

Manner

Then he'd jumped to his feet **as if he'd been bitten by a snake**, shouting, 'You're a virgin!'

Comparison

She asked Mrs Phipps, **as** delicately **as she could**.

Concession

It is bad to be a fantasist, **although sometimes it may not be that bad**.

Condition

If you start thinking about this game it will drive you crazy.

Conditional clauses

This important group of adverbial clauses deals with situations that are largely or completely hypothetical. They nearly always begin with the word *if*. There are six main kinds of conditional:

1. For example, the equilibrium between liquid and vapour is upset **if the temperature is increased**.
    (General rule, or law of nature: it always happens.)

2. **If you start thinking about this game** it will drive you crazy.
    (Open future condition: it may or may not happen.)

3. ***But if you really wanted to be on Malibu Beach,*** *you'd be there.*
    (Unlikely future condition: it probably won't happen.)

4. ***If I were you***, *I would go to the conference centre itself and ask to see someone in security.*
    (Impossible future condition: it could never happen.)

5. *'I would have resigned **if they had made the decision themselves,'** she said.*
    (Impossible past condition: it didn't happen.)

6. ***If he had been working for three days and three nights*** *then it was in the suit he was wearing now...*
    (Unknown past condition: we don't know the facts.)

At least this is how the language is supposed to work! There are a lot of native speakers who either do not understand how all these conditional forms work, or fail to use them correctly.

That applies to a lot of subordinate clause forms and functions. When someone writes in a childish or over-simplified way it is frequently because they do not have a proper understanding of, or control over, subordination.

PART C

Glossary

Numbers in the left-hand column point to the main explanations in Parts A and B.

absolute
51–52
The base form of an adjective (e.g. *happy*) which is contrasted with the COMPARATIVE (*happier*) and the SUPERLATIVE (*happiest*).

abstract noun
17
A noun that refers to an idea or something else that cannot be experienced using the five senses. The opposite of CONCRETE.

active voice
31–32
79–80
TRANSITIVE VERBS (verbs that are followed by an OBJECT) can be used in two ways, active and PASSIVE. They usually describe some kind of action in which there is an actor, and something that is affected by the action.

ACTIVE: *Google has fixed the Internet!*
Here the word *Google* is the SUBJECT and refers to the actor. The words *the Internet* form the OBJECT and refer to the thing affected by the action. The action is referred to by the ACTIVE VERB *has fixed*.

PASSIVE: *The Internet has been fixed by Google!*
Now the thing affected by the action becomes the subject and the original actor becomes the agent. The VERB becomes PASSIVE: *has been fixed*.

The active is much more common than the passive, which tends to be reserved for special situations such as formal English and scientific reports.

adjective
22–24
50–52
Adjectives help to narrow the meaning of nouns, by giving further information. They are normally used before the noun, which they are said to MODIFY:

a ***large green*** *caterpillar*

This ATTRIBUTIVE use is contrasted with the second main use of adjectives, which is after verbs such as *to be* when they provide further information about the subject.

*The caterpillar was **green**.*

This use is described as PREDICATIVE.

Adjectives can be QUALITATIVE or CLASSIFYING. Qualitative adjectives are GRADABLE: they have a COMPARATIVE and a SUPERLATIVE form (*happy–happier–happiest*, or *excitable–more excitable–most excitable*); and they can be modified by ADVERBS such as 'rather'. Classifying adjectives – like *unique* – are not normally gradable.

adjective phrase
83–84

A group of words built on an adjective HEADWORD is an adjective phrase. The headword can be PREMODIFIED, typically by an intensifying adverb:

> **very** *interesting*, **remarkably** *tedious*

It can also be POSTMODIFIED:

> *as* interesting **as ever,** *tedious* **for everyone**

adjunct
61–62
93–94

An ADVERBIAL that adds information to a clause. Typically adjuncts provide information about:

❑ place
A cat lay **outside the front door**.

❑ time
At about 1.40 pm *cars started to appear.*

❑ manner
It was discovered **by chance**.

❑ cause
Even people with adequate heating may not use it **because of the cost**.

❑ purpose
In fact I think she will live forever **just to spite me**.

❑ condition
Men with mature faces were judged to be leaders and dominant, **if rather cold**.

❑ concession
In spite of the risks *the challenge for hackers remains.*

adverb
33–38
60–63

A single word that can perform any of the roles of an ADVERBIAL:

> *Letty and I met* **there**.

> *Something awful happened* **yesterday**.

Adverbs also occur in ADJECTIVE PHRASES and ADVERB PHRASES. They are used to MODIFY the adjective or adverb:

> *They are* **extremely** *heavy.*

adverb phrase   A PHRASE based on an ADVERB HEADWORD. The adverb
60, 85   can be:

❑ premodified
*The man was driving **very** **fast**.*

❑ postmodified
*You follow **as** **fast** **as you can**.*

❑ or both
*It is all happening **too** **fast** **for us to take anything
quite for granted**.*

adverbial   A clause element which provides additional information
33–38   or helps to make a text cohere. An adverbial can be:
61–63
92–94   ❑ a single ADVERB

❑ an ADVERB PHRASE

❑ a PREPOSITIONAL PHRASE

❑ a NOUN PHRASE

❑ a SUBORDINATE CLAUSE.

Adverbials can be divided into:

❑ CONJUNCTS

❑ DISJUNCTS

❑ ADJUNCTS

adverbial clause   Adverbial clauses can express a variety of different
41–42   meanings:
102–104
❑ place
*They ought to go back **where they belong**.*

❑ time
*This was **after David had split up with Hermione**.*

❑ reason
*Some had already left **because pay was so far in
arrears**.*

❑ purpose
*He tried to pull Caspar with him s**o that they would be
hidden by a tree**...*

> ❑ result
> *...the stock did not include paste **so they were up until the early hours, matching and fastening the wallpaper on with drawing pins***.

> ❑ condition
> ***If the information is missing**, then contact the organiser to find out.*

> ❑ concession
> ***Although she did not go out of her way to make known her sexual identity,** she also did not hide it.*

> ❑ manner
> *My heart was behaving **as if I were going before a judge.***

affix A group of letters added to a word STEM which change its meaning or use. So in the word *unbelievable* the affix *un-* has been added to *believable* to change the meaning; the affix *-able* has been added to *believe* to change it from a verb to an adjective. Affixes that come at the front of the word are called PREFIXES; those that come at the back are called SUFFIXES.

agreement Verbs have to agree with their subject in NUMBER and
9, 58 PERSON. For example:

NUMBER	PRONOUN	*walk*	*be*
SINGULAR	*I*	*walk*	*am*
	you	*walk*	*are*
	he/she/it	*walks*	*is*
PLURAL	*we*	*walk*	*are*
	you	*walk*	*are*
	they	*walk*	*are*

Agreement is also called CONCORD.

apposition The use of one noun phrase to expand or explain another. The two noun phrases are placed side by side in the sentence:

 The author , *an American journalist* , *has travelled*

widely in the Balkans, and has lived in Greece.

article
The words *the*, *a*, and *an*, which are used before a noun. They are part of a larger group of words called DETERMINERS.

aspect
The VERB PHRASE can be:

❑   SIMPLE
I walk

❑   CONTINUOUS
I am walking

❑   PERFECT
I have walked

Each of these three communicates a different view of the action referred to and is called an aspect.

attributive adjective
Adjectives help to narrow the meaning of nouns, by giving further information. They are normally used before the noun, which they are said to MODIFY:

a **large green** *caterpillar*

This is the ATTRIBUTIVE use of adjectives.

See also: ADJECTIVE, PREDICATIVE.

auxiliary verb
A VERB PHRASE can consist of one verb:

*I **walked** over and **spoke** to the driver.*

or it may be made up of a group of verbs:

*I **will be speaking** to Mr Taylor privately...*

The verb phrase always contains a main verb. If there is only one verb in the phrase, then that is the main verb. If there is more than one verb in the phrase, the main verb comes at the end. The verbs that come before the main verb are called auxiliary verbs, since they 'help' convey the full meaning of the phrase. In the second example above, the auxiliary verbs are *will* and *be*.

Auxiliary verbs can be PRIMARY (*be, have, do*) or MODAL (*will, shall, would, should, may, might, can, could, must, ought to*).

backshift   When we are reporting something that someone has said, we can use direct speech and quote the actual words spoken:

> *A spokeswoman for the European Commission said, 'The complaint **will be** investigated.'*

Alternatively we can use reported speech:

> *A spokeswoman for the European Commission said that the complaint **would be** investigated.*

In reported speech the TENSE of the verbs used in direct speech is shifted back in time to fit the tenses of the report. So *is* becomes *was*, *will* becomes *would*, and so on. This phenomenon is sometimes known as backshift.

cardinal numeral   Numerals (or numbers) have these forms:

CARDINAL	*one, two, fifteen, ninety-three*
ORDINAL	*first, second, twentieth, ninety-third*
FRACTION	*half, one third, one twentieth*

Cardinals can be used as DETERMINERS:

> *There are **twenty-seven** people on the stage at any one time.*

or as PRONOUNS:

> *We took **ten** of the top trekkers through their paces.*

case   English PRONOUNS change their form according to the way in which they are used in a sentence. There are three cases:

SUBJECTIVE	OBJECTIVE	POSSESSIVE
I	*me*	*mine*
you	*you*	*yours*
he/she/it	*him/her/it*	*his/hers/its*
we	*us*	*ours*
you	*you*	*yours*
they	*them*	*theirs*

In some languages nouns also INFLECT to show subjective and objective cases, but this does not happen in English. English does have a POSSESSIVE case for nouns. This is shown by adding 's to singular nouns and plural nouns that do not end in s, and by adding an apostrophe to plural nouns ending in s.

classifying adjectives
22–24
51

A group of adjectives that help to define a NOUN by providing information about the group or class it refers to. Examples are:

agricultural   annual   medical   pregnant

Classifying adjectives cannot normally be graded: you cannot describe one event as *more annual* than another. On the other hand some classifying adjectives can also be used to describe the qualities of something or someone. The adjective *rural*, for example, is a classifying adjective in the phrase *people living in rural areas* and cannot be graded or premodified. On the other hand it can be in sentences such as:

*…they obviously came from some **very rural** place in the Apennines.*

clause
86–96

A grammatical element that is situated on the level between a PHRASE and a SENTENCE:

SENTENCE	When her husband died she became withdrawn.	
CLAUSE	her husband died	she became withdrawn
PHRASE	her husband	died

In a SIMPLE SENTENCE there is only one clause; MULTIPLE SENTENCES consist of two or more clauses. Multiple sentences can be COMPOUND or COMPLEX.

clause elements
86–94

CLAUSES can be made up of five elements:

❑ SUBJECT

❑ VERB

❑ OBJECT

❑ COMPLEMENT

☐ ADVERBIAL

clause patterns
8–16
95–96

English has seven clause patterns:

They are:

SUBJECT	VERB		
The war	has ended.		

SUBJECT	VERB	OBJECT	
I	forgot	the departmental meeting.	

SUBJECT	VERB	INDIRECT OBJECT	DIRECT OBJECT
He	bought	me	a brandy

SUBJECT	VERB	SUBJECT COMPLEMENT	
Anthony Evans	is	a musician.	

SUBJECT	VERB	OBJECT	OBJECT COMPLEMENT
Psychology	makes	him	happy.

SUBJECT	VERB	ADVERBIAL	
Jessy	lives	in Zambia.	

SUBJECT	VERB	OBJECT	ADVERBIAL
Jackie	put	his head	on one side.

collective noun   A NOUN that refers to a group of individuals, such as:

army   audience   committee   government   public

Although these are SINGULAR nouns, they can be followed by a singular or a PLURAL verb:

*The whole audience **was** astounded and it didn't go down very well.*

*Behind us in the auditorium the show was about to begin, and the audience **were** in their seats.*

The choice of number depends on how the speaker sees the audience. In the first example the audience is seen as a unit, while in the second the speaker is thinking of a group of separate individuals.

common noun
17, 48

Nouns can be divided into two groups:

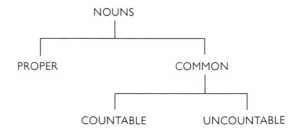

All nouns that are not PROPER NOUNS are described as common nouns.

See also: COUNTABLE, UNCOUNTABLE.

comparative
23, 51–52

All QUALITATIVE ADJECTIVES have three forms:

ABSOLUTE	COMPARATIVE	SUPERLATIVE
tall	*taller*	*tallest*
good	*better*	*best*
attractive	*more attractive*	*most attractive*

The comparative is used to compare two items:

*The pot was **taller** than a man...*

If there are more than two, then the superlative is used:

*Rachel was used to being the **tallest** woman in a room.*

complement
12–13
90–91

A clause element that completes (complements) the meaning of either the SUBJECT or the OBJECT:

SUBJECT	VERB	SUBJECT COMPLEMENT	
Anthony Evans	*is*	*a musician.*	

SUBJECT	VERB	OBJECT	OBJECT COMPLEMENT
Psychology	*makes*	*him*	*happy.*

A complement can be:

❏ an ADJECTIVE

❏ an ADJECTIVE PHRASE

❏ a NOUN

❏ a NOUN PHRASE

❏ a PRONOUN (very rare for the object complement).

complex sentence
40–42
100–104

A SENTENCE that contains at least two CLAUSES. One of these is the MAIN CLAUSE; the others are SUBORDINATE CLAUSES. For example:

SUBORDINATE CLAUSE	MAIN CLAUSE	SUBORDINATE CLAUSE
	The cards and flowers arrived	*when I got there.*
Whoever had done this	*wished him harm.*	

The way to tell a subordinate clause from a main clause is that within the sentence subordinate clauses can be replaced by a single word or a phrase and the sentence will still be grammatically sound (although the meaning may change):

The cards and flowers arrived	*when I got there.*
	afterwards.

Within the whole complex sentence each subordinate clause acts as a CLAUSE ELEMENT. For example:

The cards and flowers	*arrived*	*when I got there.*
SUBJECT	VERB	ADVERBIAL

compound sentence
40, 99

A sentence that contains two or more MAIN CLAUSES, which are joined by a CO-ORDINATING CONJUNCTION:

But they do exist	and	they can be found.
MAIN CLAUSE	CO-ORDINATING	MAIN CLAUSE

compound word A word made by combining two other words. For example:

bookcase   go-between   paper knife

As these examples show, some compounds are written as a single word, some are linked by a hyphen, while others can be written as two separate nouns.

concession An adverbial clause of concession is one which
103 expresses the idea: 'In spite of X, Y is true'. For example:

> **Although acrylic varnishes are dry in about 30 minutes**, *they continue to harden over a period of 24–48 hours…*

Concession can also be expressed in:

❑   NON-FINITE CLAUSES
*Haci Osman of Sakaltutan had failed to produce children of his own **in spite of trying four different wives.***

❑   VERBLESS CLAUSES
***Although very nervous**, he was open and defenceless when dealing with others in any teaching situation...*

concord Another term for AGREEMENT.

concrete noun A NOUN which refers to a person, place, or thing which
17 can be experienced through one or more of the five senses.

See also: ABSTRACT NOUN.

conditional A conditional SENTENCE is one which deals with
103–104 something that is hypothetical: 'If X, then Y.' Conditional sentences contain a SUBORDINATE conditional CLAUSE, which usually begins with *if*, and a MAIN CLAUSE.

There are six main types of conditional sentence:

1.   *For example, the equilibrium between liquid and vapour is upset **if the temperature is increased**.* (General rule, or law of nature: it always happens.)

2. ***If you start thinking about this game*** *it will drive
    you crazy.*
    (Open future condition: it may or may not happen.)

3. *But **if you really wanted to be on Malibu Beach,**
    you'd be there.*
    (Unlikely future condition: it probably won't hap-
    pen.)

4. ***If I were you***, *I would go to the conference centre itself
    and ask to see someone in security.*
    (Impossible future condition: it could never hap-
    pen.)

5. *'I would have resigned **if they had made the decision
    themselves,**' she said.*
    (Impossible past condition: it didn't happen.)

6. ***If he had been working for three days and three
    nights*** *then it was in the suit he was wearing now...*
    (Unknown past condition: we don't know the facts.)

conjunct   An ADVERBIAL that helps to link the meaning of one SEN-
61–63   TENCE to another. In the sentences that follow the con-
92–93   juncts are in bold type.

> *We wish to be free to do as we like without harming
> others and without interference from others. We
> **also** allow the state to stop us from doing things
> that harm ourselves. **In addition** we empower the
> state to protect us from threats from outside the
> country.*

Conjuncts can be single words:

also	*alternatively*	*besides*	*finally*
first(ly)	*however*	*moreover*	*next*
otherwise	*similarly*	*then*	*therefore*

or phrases:

in addition	*because of this*	*in spite of that*
in the end	*to begin with*	*in the same way*

conjunction
69–70

We use conjunctions to join together two grammatical elements. A conjunction like *and* can join two single words:

> Then **you** [*and*] **I** *would both be sorry.*

or two phrases:

> *But he denied possessing* **the vegetable** [*and*] **the iron bar** *as imitation firearms.*

or two clauses:

> **The door swung back slowly, silently,** [*and*] **he went in.**

Conjunctions can be of two kinds:

- ❏ CO-ORDINATING

- ❏ SUBORDINATING

connective
63
157–159

This is not a grammatical term, but is included here because it is sometimes used to refer to the way in which texts are constructed. It covers a large group of expressions, which are grammatically distinct:

- ❏ ADVERBS

- ❏ ADVERB PHRASES

- ❏ ADVERBIAL CLAUSES

- ❏ CONJUNCTS

- ❏ DISJUNCTS

- ❏ CONJUNCTIONS

continuous aspect
78

The VERB PHRASE in a CLAUSE provides two kinds of information:

- ❏ TIME
  PAST — PRESENT — FUTURE

- ❏ ASPECT
  SIMPLE — CONTINUOUS — PERFECT

The continuous aspect emphasises that the activity referred to by the verb goes on over a period of time. For example:

As *I **was going*** to St Ives
I met a man with seven wives…

Here the single event (*I met*) occurred while something else was going on (*I was going*).

There are six continuous tenses:

PRESENT CONTINUOUS	*I am walking*
PRESENT PERFECT CONTINU-OUS	*I have been walking*
PAST CONTINUOUS	*I was walking*
PAST PERFECT CONTINUOUS	*I had been walking*
FUTURE CONTINUOUS	*I shall be walking*
FUTURE PERFECT CONTINU-OUS	*I shall have been walking*

co-ordinating conjunction
40, 69

A conjunction that links two grammatical elements:

❑ WORDS
*men **and** women*
*red **or** green*

❑ PHRASES
*homosexual men **and** lesbian women*
*berry red **or** holly green*

❑ CLAUSES
*You can do it on your own **or** you can get together with family and friends.*

The commonest co-ordinating conjunctions are:

and   or   but

copular verb   See LINKING VERB.

countable noun
17, 48–49

COMMON NOUNS can be divided into countable and UNCOUNTABLE. Countable nouns are those which refer to things that can be counted:

one bus   five buses
a man   two men

By definition, countable nouns have a SINGULAR and a PLURAL form.

declarative
87–88, 97

One of four SENTENCE types. (The others are INTERROGATIVE, EXCLAMATIVE, and IMPERATIVE.) Declarative sentences are those which are used to make statements.

demonstrative pronoun
66

The four demonstrative pronouns are:

> *this*　　*that*　　*these*　*those*

They are used to refer to things spatially. *This/these* refer to things that are close at hand, while *that/those* refer to things that are further away:

> *No sex in the afternoon. **This** is Edinburgh after all.*

In speech and writing they can also be used to refer to things that are closer to or further away from the topic being discussed.

derivational morphology

Forming new words by adding a PREFIX or a SUFFIX to a STEM:

un	*success*	*ful*
PREFIX	STEM	SUFFIX

determiner
20–21, 67

A group of words that are used before NOUNS to give them more definition. The following three SENTENCES demonstrate how this works:

> **Prisons** *have play areas for children.*
>
> **The** *prisons have play areas for children.*
>
> **Some** *prisons have play areas for children.*
>
> **Few** *prisons have play areas for children.*

The, some, and *few* are all determiners.

The commonest determiners are:

> *a*　　　*an*　　*the*
> *this*　　*that*　　*these*　*those*
> *some*　*any*　　*no*
> *my*　　*our*　　*your*　*his*　　*her*　*its*　　*their*
> *many*　*few*　　*little*　*much*
> *other*　*last*　　*next*

There are also determiners which can come before these words. These include:

> all   both   half
> twice   such   many

Cardinal numbers (*three, twenty*) and ordinals (*fifth, last*) also function as determiners, but come after the main group above:

> ***All the* five** *Dhyani Buddhas are said to have originated from Vajrasattva himself.*

dialect   A distinctive form of a language spoken by a specific group of people, usually defined geographically. Dialects differ from each other in pronunciation, vocabulary and GRAMMAR.

direct object   The OBJECT of a CLAUSE or SENTENCE:
11–12
54, 89

- ❏ normally comes after the VERB

- ❏ is a NOUN or 'noun-like thing'

- ❏ usually refers to a different person, thing or idea from the SUBJECT.

- ❏ very often tells us about a person or thing that is

    - • affected by the action of the verb, **or**
    - • 'acted upon' in some way.

Some clauses have two objects:

Two years later he bought	*my mother*	*a new car...*
	OBJECT 1	OBJECT 2

These two objects serve different purposes in the sentence. Object 2 is directly affected by the action of giving: we can imagine the subject going to the showroom, buying the car and handing it over to *my mother*. Object 1, *my mother*, is not so directly affected by his action: she receives the car and may be pleased to do so, but that is all. So object 2 is referred to as the DIRECT OBJECT, while object 1 is the INDIRECT OBJECT:

Two years later he bought	my mother	a new car...
	INDIRECT OBJECT	DIRECT OBJECT

disjunct
61–63
92–93

A SENTENCE ADVERBIAL that a speaker uses to make a comment on what s/he is saying. For example:

> *Ironically, Mike Roberts is one person who welcomed the drought earlier this summer.*

> *In actual fact the two fish are not that alike.*

As in these two examples, disjuncts can be a single word (an ADVERB) or a phrase (usually a PREPOSITIONAL PHRASE).

ditransitive verb

A verb that can take both a DIRECT and an INDIRECT OBJECT.

dummy subject

A CLAUSE SUBJECT that has no real meaning or reference, but which is just used to begin the SENTENCE:

> *It only needs one person to pass on an infection.*

> *There are mountains nearby.*

either/or question
97

A question in which the speaker expects one of two possible answers:

> *Do you need to be the one in charge of all decision making, or would you rather have someone else make the major decisions?*

embedding

Sometimes a phrase or clause contains another phrase or clause within it. The phrase or clause that is contained in this way is said to be embedded. For example:

three-quarters of patients | who completed treatment

NOUN PHRASE   RELATIVE CLAUSE

exclamative
8, 98

A sentence form used to express exclamations:

> *What a difference a few precious centimetres can make in this game of high stakes.*

> *How strange it is, strange and sad, to see all these tropical faces amid the slush and dirty snow…*

Full exclamative sentences begin with *What...* or *How...*

finite clause
7

A CLAUSE that contains a FINITE VERB.

finite verb
42–43
79

A full CLAUSE must contain a finite verb. This is a VERB which shows:

❑ TENSE
*They **went** home.*

❑ NUMBER
*We **are** cousins.*

If the VERB PHRASE consists of more than one verb, then the first verb in it must be finite:

SUBJECT	VERB PHRASE		OBJECT
We	are	going to visit	the Tower of London.
	FINITE VERB		

focus (adjunct)

An ADVERBIAL that is used to focus attention on a particular section of a CLAUSE:

*Police officers insist that most of the killings are drug-related, **especially** in Rio, where minors are employed as delivery boys and armed lookouts by traffickers.*

*They are free **only** when they are electing members of parliament.*

future continuous tense
77

A verb tense that refers to the future and emphasises that the action described goes on over a period of time:

*So we **will be working** to provide better services geared to people's needs.*

future perfect continuous tense
77

The continuous form of the FUTURE PERFECT TENSE (see below):

*This last week McGeechan **will have been working** on videos.*

future perfect tense
77

A tense in which the speaker imagines himself/herself in the future, looking back in time:

*Bill feels that the recruitment campaign **will have succeeded** if it results in a significant increase in the numbers of women applying to become fire-fighters.*

future tense
77

A VERB TENSE that refers to the future. It is formed using *will* or *shall* followed by the verb STEM:

*Kathleen **will know** what to do.*

The other common way of forming a verb phrase to refer to the future is to use *going to*:

*Where is Britain **going to build** its next major airport?*

See also SIMPLE FUTURE TENSE.

gerund

The *-ing* form of the VERB used as a NOUN:

***Refusing** to speak is an exercise of the right to silence.*

*They are hanging on by **refusing** to pay suppliers.*

grading
23, 51

QUALITATIVE ADJECTIVES refer to the qualities of something or someone. So, for example, we can say,

*That was an **unusual** film.*

Adjectives like *unusual* can be graded: we can have more or less of the qualities they refer to. We can say the film was:

***rather** unusual*

***slightly** unusual*

***extremely** unusual.*

As the examples show, adjectives are graded by placing an ADVERB in front of them. CLASSIFYING ADJECTIVES cannot be graded.

grammar
2

The formal study of how a language works. There are two main strands:

❏ SYNTAX
the ways in which words are ordered to form PHRASES, CLAUSES, and SENTENCES

❑   MORPHOLOGY
how the form of words is changed according to how
they are used.

grapheme   A letter or combination of letters used to represent a
PHONEME. So the following are all graphemes:

t   ai   sh   z

head   See HEADWORD.

headword   The individual word on which a PHRASE is built up. In a
71   NOUN PHRASE it is a NOUN:

the classic prawn **cocktail**

In a VERB PHRASE it is the MAIN VERB:

Your computer | *will* ***complete*** | *the connection.*

In a PREPOSITIONAL PHRASE it is the opening PREPOSITION:

in *the box*

It is sometimes also called the HEAD of the phrase.

imperative   If we wish to make commands or give orders we use a
8, 98   SENTENCE form that differs in one important way from a
DECLARATIVE sentence:

❑   DECLARATIVE
You put it on the table.

❑   IMPERATIVE
Put it on the table.

The subject of the sentence, *you*, is not stated, but is
understood. Most imperatives are second person like this,
but it is also possible to have first person imperatives:

Let us look *at this more closely.*

indefinite pronoun   A PRONOUN which, as its name suggests, allows the
19, 66   speaker to be imprecise about exactly who or what is
referred to. The commonest are:

some	*someone*	*somebody*	*something*
any	*anyone*	*anybody*	*anything*
none	*no one*	*nobody*	*nothing*
all	*everyone*	*everybody*	*everything*
either	*neither*	*both*	*each*

indirect object   The OBJECT of a CLAUSE or SENTENCE:
11–12, 54
❏   normally comes after the VERB

❏   is a NOUN or noun-like thing

❏   usually refers to a different person, thing or idea from the subject.

❏   very often tells us about a person or thing that is

•   affected by the action of the verb, **or**
•   'acted upon' in some way.

Some clauses have two objects:

Two years later he bought	my mother	a new car...
	OBJECT 1	OBJECT 2

These two objects serve different purposes in the sentence. Object 2 is directly affected by the action of giving: we can imagine the subject going to the showroom, buying the car and handing it over to *my mother*. Object 1, *my mother*, is not so directly affected by his action: she receives the car and may be pleased to do so, but that is all. So object 2 is referred to as the DIRECT OBJECT, while object 1 is the INDIRECT OBJECT:

Two years later he bought	my mother	a new car...
	INDIRECT OBJECT	DIRECT OBJECT

infinitive   The STEM of the VERB on which the other parts of the
58   verb are based:

STEM/INFINITIVE	talk	run	go
PRESENT PARTICIPLE	talking	running	going
PAST PARTICIPLE	talked	run	gone
PRESENT TENSE	talk(s)	run(s)	go(es)
PAST TENSE	talked	ran	went

In VERB PHRASES it can be preceded by *to*:

*I would like **to add** another catfish.*

inflection
25, 57

When the form of a word is changed according to its use in a sentence, this is called inflection. Examples are:

❏ PLURALS
one table, several tables
one mouse, three mice

❏ TENSE
I hope, I hoped
we go, we went

inflectional morphology

When the form of a word is changed it is described as MORPHOLOGY. Inflectional morphology describes changes which occur because of the way a word is used in a SENTENCE.

See also INFLECTION.

intensifier
34–35
60–61

An ADVERB which modifies the meaning of an ADJECTIVE or another adverb. For example:

*The occupants of The Haunt were all **rather** peculiar.*

*Something **very** strange is happening.*

interrogative
7, 97

A SENTENCE form used to ask questions. There are three types:

yes/no questions

As their name suggests, these expect the reply *yes* or *no*:

Were the instruments messed up?

The word order of a DECLARATIVE sentence has to be changed to form this type of sentence. If there is an AUXILIARY VERB it is placed in front of the SUBJECT, as in the example above. If the declarative sentence would not contain an auxiliary, then one is provided: *do, does,* or *did,* and the MAIN VERB changes accordingly:

DECLARATIVE: *He **went** to school as usual.*

INTERROGATIVE: ***Did** he **go** to school as usual?*

wh- questions

Sometimes called 'open' questions, these invite a wide range of possible answers. They generally begin with one of the following:

who(m)   whose   which   what
why   when   where   how

The sentence structure depends on which question word is used. If the question word forms the subject of the sentence, then the structure is the same as a declarative sentence:

Who said that?

In other cases, the word order is changed like this:

You last saw your father

When did you last see your father?

either/or

Some questions offer the respondent two possible answers. For example:

Does the benefit from education accrue to parents or children?

interrogative pronoun
19, 66

A PRONOUN used to form questions:

who   whom   whose   which   what

intransitive
27, 55–56

An intransitive verb is one which is not followed by an OBJECT, as opposed to a TRANSITIVE VERB which does have an object. Examples of intransitive verbs are:

arrive   faint   pause   weep

Quite a large number of verbs can be both transitive and intransitive. For example the verb *meet* in the following sentences:

*When you first **meet** someone, assume you will **meet** them again.* (TRANSITIVE)

*They all **meet** later, and Kevin gets his revenge.* (INTRANSITIVE)

inversion Reversing two elements in a clause. The most frequent example of this occurs in the formation of *yes/no* QUESTIONS:

The instruments   were   messed up.

Were   the instruments   messed up?

irregular verb A verb which does not follow the normal pattern when
26, 58–59 forming the PAST TENSE and PAST PARTICIPLE. For example:

STEM	PAST TENSE	PAST PARTICIPLE
ring	*rang*	*rung*
beat	*beat*	*beaten*
hit	*hit*	*hit*

lexical Relating to vocabulary, and specifically to open class
27 words: NOUNS, VERBS, ADJECTIVES, and ADVERBS.

lexical morphology The study of how new words are formed by adding
PREFIXES or SUFFIXES to existing words. For example:

un + attractive ⟶ unattractive

unattractive + ness ⟶ unattractiveness

lexical pattern See WORD FAMILY.

lexical verb See MAIN VERB.

linking verb A VERB that is followed by a COMPLEMENT. The commonest
27, 55–56 linking verb is *be*. Others are *seem*, and *become*. Another
term for linking verb is copula, or COPULAR VERB.

main clause A SENTENCE can contain one or more CLAUSES. If there
40, 100 is only one clause in a sentence, then that is the
main clause and the sentence is described as a SIMPLE
SENTENCE. If the sentence contains more than one clause
(a MULTIPLE SENTENCE), then it can be one of two types:

❑   COMPOUND

❑   COMPLEX

A COMPOUND SENTENCE consists of two or more main
clauses linked by CO-ORDINATING CONJUNCTIONS:

She had wanted to work at the Children's Hospital, but there were no vacancies.

If you remove the conjunctions, each of the main clauses can stand on its own as a simple sentence:

She had wanted to work at the Children's Hospital.

There were no vacancies.

A COMPLEX SENTENCE is built up on the main clause, and other clauses are subordinate to it:

If the Conservatives should perform poorly in the local elections the Telegraph *and the* Mail *may let fly.*

Within the complex sentence the SUBORDINATE CLAUSES fulfil the roles of clause components within the main clause:

SUBORDINATE CLAUSE	MAIN CLAUSE
If it's on the Internet,	*it must be true.*
ADVERBIAL CLAUSE (CONDITION)	

main verb
26–27
53–56
76

Every CLAUSE must contain a main verb. If the VERB PHRASE consists of only one word then that word is normally a full verb (although there are a few exceptions). Main verbs are sometime called LEXICAL VERBS because they have a meaning you can look up in a dictionary. They are contrasted with AUXILIARY VERBS.

mass noun See UNCOUNTABLE NOUN.

metalanguage The technical language we use to talk about language itself and how it works.

modal auxiliary
28, 57

AUXILIARY VERBS are verbs which combine with the MAIN VERB to form a VERB PHRASE. The modal auxiliaries are:

shall will should would
can could
may might
must
ought (to)

These verbs are used to build verb phrases which refer to possible events rather than actual events, as is shown by the following pair of sentences:

*Ask him if he thinks I **have visited** Mr Conchis.*

*Ask him if he thinks I **might visit** Mr Conchis.*

modifier
21–22
72–75

A word or group of words which changes the meaning of the HEADWORD of a PHRASE. The modifier can come before or after the headword. In the examples that follow the modifiers are in bold type.

*Then there were his butterflies, which I suppose were **rather** beautiful.*

*Another day and they passed the **large green** tents **of the Red Cross**.*

modify

To alter the meaning of the HEADWORD of a PHRASE by placing MODIFIERS before or after it.

morpheme

The smallest unit in the language that can convey meaning. This is often a word, but it may be smaller than a word. For example, in the word *unusual*, there are two morphemes: *un + usual*.

morphology

The study of the structure of words. INFLECTIONAL MORPHOLOGY deals with the ways in which the form of words changes according to the requirements of GRAMMAR. LEXICAL MORPHOLOGY covers how the meaning of a word can be changed by adding a PREFIX or a SUFFIX.

multiple sentence

A SENTENCE that contains more than one CLAUSE.

nominal clause
41, 102

A CLAUSE within a COMPLEX SENTENCE that works like a NOUN, PRONOUN, or NOUN PHRASE. The examples that follow show how nominal clauses can be reduced to a pronoun or a noun phrase.

MAIN CLAUSE	NOMINAL CLAUSE
They were told	*that the prisoners were not there any more.*
	nothing. (PRONOUN)

NOMINAL CLAUSE	MAIN CLAUSE
What I actually needed to do	*was somehow to disappear.*
My need (NOUN PHRASE)	

Nominal clauses are also referred to as NOUN CLAUSES.

non-count noun   See UNCOUNTABLE.

non-finite clause   A CLAUSE that does not contain a FINITE VERB. A non-finite
43   clause contains a VERB in one of the following forms:

1.   *to* + INFINITIVE
     *He was not, I knew, a person **to talk about himself or
     his emotions.***

2.   PRESENT PARTICIPLE
     *Which former president owned a pet goat **while living
     in the White House**?*

3.   PAST PARTICIPLE
     *Kate, **freed at last**, was discreetly rubbing her arm.*

non-restrictive relative   A RELATIVE CLAUSE which does not restrict or define the
clause   NOUN which it MODIFIES. If you remove it, the sentence
101–102   still works. For example:

> *Senator Joe Lieberman, **who won re-election as a
> third-party candidate after a hard race against
> challenger Ned Lamont**, has a message for his
> Senate colleagues.*

If you remove the relative clause the sentence still works
without a major change of meaning:

> *Senator Joe Lieberman has a message for his
> Senate colleagues.*

The relative clause does not restrict *Senator Joe
Liebermann*. Compare that with the following example:

> *A senator **who is found guilty of treason, indict-
> able offence, or any 'infamous crime,'** also loses
> his or her seat.*

In this example the relative clause clearly does restrict

senator. If we remove it we radically alter the meaning of the sentence:

A senator also loses his or her seat.

noun
17–18
47–49

A very large WORD CLASS. Nouns satisfy all or most of these criteria:

❑ They can be plural or singular:
one cigar; two cigars

❑ They can stand as the headword of a noun phrase:
a cigar called Hamlet

❑ They can be modified by an adjective:
a large cigar

The majority of nouns refer to people, places, things, and ideas.

noun clause See NOMINAL CLAUSE.

noun phrase
20–22
72–75

A PHRASE built up on a noun HEADWORD. For example:

an inspiring leader with a never-say-die attitude

Noun phrases can act as the SUBJECT, OBJECT, or COMPLEMENT of a CLAUSE. They can also form part of PREPOSITIONAL PHRASES. Their main components are:

❑ DETERMINER
an *inspiring leader with a never-say-die attitude*

❑ PREMODIFIER
*an **inspiring** leader with a never-say-die attitude*

❑ POSTMODIFIER
*an inspiring leader **with a never-say-die attitude***

number
47, 58

SINGULAR or PLURAL. In English NOUNS, PRONOUNS and VERBS can show number.

object
10–12
54, 89
95

A CLAUSE ELEMENT. The object of a CLAUSE normally comes after the VERB and refers to someone or something different from the SUBJECT:

*Martin telephoned **his wife**.*

The exception to this is when the object is a REFLEXIVE PRONOUN:

*Martin hurt **himself**.*

The object may be a SINGLE NOUN, PRONOUN, or NOUN PHRASE, or an ADJECTIVE that is being used as a noun:

*I hate **blue**.*

or a verb GERUND (the *-ing* form, used as a noun):

*We love **skating**.*

object complement
13, 90–91
95

A CLAUSE ELEMENT which completes the meaning of the OBJECT. For example:

In March 2002 the President of the Czech Republic appointed her a Justice and Deputy Chief Justice of the Czech Constitutional Court.

*I told him all that left me **cold**.*

The object complement is usually:

❑   an ADJECTIVE or ADJECTIVE PHRASE

❑   a NOUN or NOUN PHRASE

ordinal

A numeral or word that indicates the placing of someone or something in a rank order:

*Argentina finished in **sixth** place.*

*In August 1939 he escaped with his family on the **last** but one ship to leave Hamburg.*

parenthesis

If we wish to include in a sentence additional, but non-essential information, we can do this by placing it in parenthesis:

*Once submitted to a search engine, your site will be automatically added to **(or 'crawled into')** its database whenever it's next updated*

*Mr Badran**, a former intelligence chief,** has bowed to public pressure to bring in democratic reforms...*

*They prioritize what the boss wants to prioritize, or – **perhaps worse** – give everything on the site equal weight.*

The words in parenthesis can be removed without altering the essential grammar of the sentence. As these examples show, they are marked off by the use of commas, dashes, or brackets.

part of speech   An older name for WORD CLASS.

participle   A part of the VERB. There are two participles: PRESENT and
26, 58   PAST.

- ❏   PRESENT PARTICIPLE: *walking, ringing*

- ❏   PAST PARTICIPLE: *walked, rung*

passive voice   TRANSITIVE verbs can be in one of two voices: ACTIVE and
31–32   passive. In the active voice the normal clause pattern is:
79–80
SUBJECT — VERB — OBJECT

For example:

SUBJECT	VERB	OBJECT
Garibaldi	*defeated*	*the Neapolitain army.*

In the passive the object becomes the subject and the
original subject becomes the agent, preceded by the
word *by*:

SUBJECT	VERB	AGENT
The Neapolitain army	*was defeated*	*by Garibaldi.*

Passive verb forms are constructed using the verb *be*
followed by the PAST PARTICIPLE:

	SIMPLE	CONTINUOUS	PERFECT	PERFECT CONTINUOUS
PAST	*he was defeated*	*he was being defeated*	*he had been defeated*	*he had been being defeated*
PRESENT	*he is defeated*	*he is being defeated*	*he has been defeated*	*he has been being defeated*
FUTURE	*he will be defeated*	*he will be being defeated*	*he will have been defeated*	*he will have been being defeated*

As the examples show, a number of these are fairly rare – even if grammatically possible.

past continuous
77

A VERB TENSE referring to the past and focusing on the fact that the action described continued over a period of time:

> Four people **were playing** bridge on a blanket spread over one end of the table.

past participle
26, 58

A part of the VERB. In REGULAR VERBS it is formed by adding -ed to the stem. IRREGULAR VERBS have a variety of forms of past participle. The past participle is used to form perfect tenses: *he has walked, he had walked,* etc. It is also used to form the PASSIVE.

past perfect
77

A verb TENSE which refers to the past with a focus on the idea that the action described is complete. For example:

> He puzzled about it when **they had left**.

Here one thing (the departure) is completed before another begins (*he puzzled about it*).

The past perfect is formed by the AUXILIARY *had*, followed by the PAST PARTICIPLE of the MAIN VERB.

past perfect continuous
77

A verb TENSE formed by the AUXILIARY VERBS *had been*, followed by the PRESENT PARTICIPLE of the MAIN VERB. It is used:

❑ to emphasise that an action in the past went on over a period of time
*Granny **had been living** with us for some time.*

❑ to contrast a continuing action in the past with a single past event
*The injured police officer **had been trying** to get drivers to slow down when he was hit by a car that lost control.*

past tense
77

One of the two 'true' grammatical tenses in English, the other being the PRESENT. In REGULAR VERBS it is formed by adding -ed to the verb STEM. Irregular verbs form the past tense in a variety of ways.

For usage, see SIMPLE PAST TENSE.

perfect aspect
78

One of three TENSE aspects, the others being SIMPLE and CONTINUOUS. The perfect aspect focuses attention on the relationship between the event described and the present, or some point in the past.

See: PRESENT PERFECT, PAST PERFECT, FUTURE PERFECT.

person

There are three persons in English. See PERSONAL PRONOUN.

personal pronoun
19, 65

A pronoun that can refer to a person, thing, or idea:

SINGULAR			
	SUBJECT	OBJECT	POSSESSIVE
1ST PERSON	*I*	*me*	*mine*
2ND PERSON	*you*	*you*	*yours*
3RD PERSON	*he/she/it*	*him/her/it*	*his/hers/its*

PLURAL			
	SUBJECT	OBJECT	POSSESSIVE
1ST PERSON	*we*	*us*	*ours*
2ND PERSON	*you*	*you*	*yours*
3RD PERSON	*they*	*them*	*theirs*

phoneme

A speech sound. Human beings are capable of making an enormous number of different sounds. Different languages make use of different selections of sounds to convey meaning. The set of meaningful sounds that are used within a language are called its phonemes. Changing one phoneme in a word either changes its meaning or makes it meaningless. If we change the initial sound of *beat* to an 'h', we produce a completely different word. If we change the 'b' to a hard 'g', we make no word at all.

English has about 44 phonemes (depending on regional variations). Phonemes do not, of course, correspond to letters: the 'sh' sound at the beginning of *sheet* is one phoneme but two letters. (See GRAPHEMES.)

phrase
71–85

A group of words or a single word that operates as a CLAUSE ELEMENT. There are five types of phrase:

- ❏ NOUN PHRASE
- ❏ VERB PHRASE
- ❏ PREPOSITIONAL PHRASE
- ❏ ADJECTIVE PHRASE
- ❏ ADVERB PHRASE

plural
47

More than one. Most NOUNS have plural forms and there are also plural forms for PERSONAL PRONOUNS. Verbs have to agree with their SUBJECT in NUMBER: *he walks, they walk*, etc.

possessive case

Most NOUNS, certain PRONOUNS and DETERMINERS have a special form to show possession:

- ❏ NOUN
  *At the turn of the century Paris caught **people's** imagination.*

- ❏ PRONOUN
  *Now everything was **hers**: the house, George's savings.*

- ❏ DETERMINER
  *Since then, **their** fortunes have changed spectacularly.*

possessive determiner
65

The possessive determiners are:

my   our   your   his   her   its   their

Sometimes these are described as POSSESSIVE PRONOUNS, but this is misleading, because PRONOUNS can stand on their own, which is what the true possessive pronouns (*mine, ours,* etc.) do. They are also sometimes called 'possessive adjectives', but again it's not a helpful description, because they don't do any of the things that true ADJECTIVES can do.

See also DETERMINER.

possessive pronoun
19, 65

The possessive pronouns are:

mine   ours   yours   his   hers   its   theirs

They can be used as follows:

- ❏ as the SUBJECT of a CLAUSE
  ***Theirs** is a life apart, as far as we are concerned.*

☐   as the OBJECT of a clause
*Without warning she reached her hand sideways and took **mine** and pressed it.*

☐   as the COMPLEMENT of a clause
*These statuettes are **hers** as well.*

☐   preceded by a PREPOSITION
*When have I ever touched anything of **yours**?*

possessives   Words which indicate that something belongs to someone are described as possessives. They are:

☐   POSSESSIVE PRONOUNS

☐   POSSESSIVE DETERMINERS

the possessive form of NOUNS, indicated by adding an
apostrophe followed by the letter 's', except in the case
of plurals which already end in 's', where the apostrophe
is placed on its own after the 's'.

postmodifier   A word or group of words that modifies a word and is
73–75   placed after it. Nouns, adjectives, and adverbs can all be
83, 85   postmodified:

*That's the task **of the moment**, in between everyday work.*

*I'm as happy **as a monkey in a banana factory**.*

*Well, you'll know soon **enough**.*

predicate   The part of a CLAUSE that follows the SUBJECT and
develops it. It contains the VERB and may also contain an
OBJECT, COMPLEMENT or ADVERBIAL.

predicative adjective   An ADJECTIVE that forms the SUBJECT COMPLEMENT of a CLAUSE:
22, 50

*Then I became **angry**.*

*It is doubtful if this detail is **authentic**.*

The other way in which adjectives are used is to MODIFY
a noun. This use is described as ATTRIBUTIVE. Most
adjectives can be used in both ways, but a few cannot.
For example, the adjective *alone* can only be used
predicatively.

prefix   An AFFIX which comes at the beginning of a word. In the
list of words below the prefixes are in bold:

*auto*biography   *counter*act   *mega*star

*mis*adventure   *para*normal   *under*achieve

premodifier
73, 83, 85

A word or group of words that modifies a word and is placed before it. NOUNS, ADJECTIVES, and ADVERBS can all be premodified:

*a **large yellow Ford Transit** van*

***extremely** effective*

preposition
68

A small(ish) class of words, many of which refer to position in space and time. They are placed before:

❑ a NOUN
*   ***beyond** hope*

❑ a PRONOUN
*   ***after** you*

❑ an ADJECTIVE (used as a noun)
*   ***in** blue*

❑ a NOUN PHRASE
*   ***after** his last performance*

❑ a CLAUSE
*   ***after** what you have just said*

They include:

about	*after*	*as*	*at*	*before*
between	*by*	*during*	*for*	*from*
in	*into*	*of*	*on*	*over*
than	*through*	*to*	*under*	*with*

prepositional phrase
37–38, 82

A phrase which begins with a PREPOSITION as its HEADWORD. For example:

in a few moments

for a lad of twelve years

Prepositional phrases are used:

❑ as an ADVERBIAL
*   ***In a few moments** they were alone.*

❑ to MODIFY a NOUN
*   *He began to make a collection **of brass rubbings**.*

❑   to modify an ADJECTIVE or ADVERB:
*Jonathan Rodriguez is doing something unusual **for a 19-year-old guy in the inner city**.*

❑   as a SUBJECT COMPLEMENT
*The critics were **over the moon**.*

preposition stranding   A term used to describe what happens when a PREPOSITION is separated (stranded) from the words that would normally be expected to follow it:

*He didn't need to ask what his sergeant was refer- ring **to**.*

Some pedants argue that you shouldn't do this, but if you don't, you end up appearing rather old-fashioned:

*He didn't need to ask **to** what his sergeant was referring.*

present continuous   A verb TENSE that refers to events taking place in
77   the present and focuses on the fact that the action continues over a period of time:

*P. J. O'Rourke **is writing** the lyrics for the new Julian Cope album.*

The present continuous is also used for future time:

A group of Japanese academics are visiting the Social Work Department, on Saturday, September 18th.

present participle   The form of the VERB made by adding *-ing* to the STEM. It
26, 58   is used in forming CONTINUOUS TENSES:

***They will be running** a minibus service on that evening.*

It can also be used as the verb in NON-FINITE CLAUSES:

***When running flat-out**, only one foot touches the ground at any one moment.*

present perfect   A VERB TENSE in which the speaker refers to an event
77   that began in the past but which is continuing into the present (or which has effects that are doing so).

*Souza **has lived** in New York for the last twenty years.*

It is also used to refer to completed events which are still important now:

> Our operating activities during the year **have achieved** a number of successes.

present perfect continuous tense
77

A verb tense which is similar to the present perfect but which emphasises that the events went on over a period of time:

> The rumour mill **has been working** overtime at the Dan Rhodes skyscraper, here in downtown Taipei.

present tense
77

In the strict grammatical sense there are only two TENSES in English: PAST and present. In this sense 'tense' is shown by a change to the form of the VERB. The present tense is formed from the STEM of the verb and -s is added for the THIRD PERSON SINGULAR, *he/she/it*:

> She **works** at Crompton's, on the industrial estate.

Confusingly the English present tense doesn't necessarily refer to present time. Its main uses are described in the entry for SIMPLE PRESENT TENSE.

primary auxiliary verb
56–57

The primary auxiliary verbs are:

> *be   have   do*

They have two uses:

❑ as MAIN VERBS
> Parading captives on the screen **is** now a routine part of war.
> The truth is that doctors **do** their best, but people's expectations are too high.
> Megan McArdle now **has** her own cool online store.

❑ as AUXILIARY VERBS
> It turned out that Gail Benson **had been** stabbed and buried alive.
> But on balance, the children think they understand the work better, and so **do** the teachers.

pronoun
18–20
64–66

A class of words consisting of seven groups:

❑ PERSONAL pronouns
(e.g. *I/you*)

- ❑ POSSESSIVE **pronouns**
  (e.g. *mine/yours*)

- ❑ REFLEXIVE **pronouns**
  (e.g. *myself/yourself*)

- ❑ DEMONSTRATIVE **pronouns**
  (e.g. *this/that*)

- ❑ INDEFINITE **pronouns**
  (e.g. *someone/no one*)

- ❑ INTERROGATIVE **pronouns**
  (e.g. *who/which*)

- ❑ RELATIVE **pronouns**
  (e.g. *who/which*)

Pronouns can be used in these ways:

- ❑ as the SUBJECT of a CLAUSE
  These *are not isolated examples.*

- ❑ as the OBJECT of a clause
  *I thought you'd had **yours** when you made **mine**.*

- ❑ as the COMPLEMENT of a clause
  *The enemy is **them**.*

- ❑ preceded by a PREPOSITION
  *Marriage is the alliance of two people, one **of whom** never remembers birthdays and the other who never forgets.*

proper noun
17, 48   Proper nouns refer to people, places, things and ideas that are unique. They are often written with initial capital letters and include:

- ❑ The names of individual people and places
  Jane, Paris

- ❑ The names of organisations, institutions, publications, films, TV programmes, pieces of music and other things that are unique
  Parliament, Hamlet

- ❑ People's titles when used to refer to an individual, with or without their personal name:
  the Professor, the President
  This does not apply when the title is used

generically:

some professors

the presidents of several EU countries

qualitative adjective
22–24, 51

ADJECTIVES fall into two groups: qualitative and CLASSIFYING. Qualitative adjectives give information about the qualities of the NOUN they modify:

*I think he's a **clever** guy.*

Qualitative adjectives can be modified by the addition of an intensifier:

*I think he's a **very clever** guy.*

*I think he's a **fairly clever** guy.*

reflexive pronoun
19, 65–66

The reflexive pronouns are:

myself   yourself   himself   herself
itself   ourselves   themselves

They refer back to someone or something already mentioned, in SENTENCES such as:

*He injured **himself** during the prank.*

*I'm not quite sure what we're letting **ourselves** in for, Sam.*

regular verb
26

A VERB which follows the normal rules for forming the PAST TENSE and the PAST PARTICIPLE, for example:

walk/walked/walked

This is in contrast to IRREGULAR VERBS, which do not follow those rules, for example:

forget/forgot/forgotten

relative adverb
74

The words *when, where,* and *why* can be used to introduce a RELATIVE CLAUSE in sentences such as:

*Kincaid introduces readers to the place **where she grew up**.*

When they are used in this way they are referred to as relative adverbs.

relative clause
41, 73–75, 101–102

A CLAUSE that MODIFIES a NOUN. Relative clauses are introduced by a RELATIVE PRONOUN:

who whom whose which that

For example:

*Three-quarters of patients **who completed treat-ment** found it helpful.*

*Think of someone **whom you admire at the moment**.*

Relative clauses can also be introduced without a relative pronoun, the so-called ZERO RELATIVE.

*The only thing **I can think about now** is being hard up.*

relative pronoun
19, 66, 74
The PRONOUNS *who, whom, whose, which, that* used to introduce RELATIVE CLAUSES.

restrictive relative clause
101–102
A RELATIVE CLAUSE that restricts or defines the NOUN it MODIFIES to the extent that removing it from the clause would radically alter its meaning:

*A senator **who is found guilty of treason, indictable offence, or any 'infamous crime,'** also loses his or her seat.*

The relative clause *who is found ... crime,'* clearly restricts the meaning of *senator*. If we remove it we radically alter the meaning of the sentence:

A senator also loses his or her seat.

On the other hand, a non-restrictive relative clause can be removed without a radical change to the meaning:

*Senator Joe Lieberman, **who won re-election as an third-party candidate after a hard race against challenger Ned Lamont**, has a message for his Senate colleagues.*

If you remove the words *who was there*, the sentence still works without a major change of meaning:

Senator Joe Lieberman has a message for his Senate colleagues.

root
See STEM.

sentence
6–8, 39–44
97–104
A grammatical unit made up of one or more FINITE CLAUSES. A SIMPLE SENTENCE contains one CLAUSE and a MULTIPLE SENTENCE contains two or more. Multiple

sentences can be COMPOUND or COMPLEX. There are four SENTENCE TYPES, each with a different communicative purpose:

❏   DECLARATIVE, for making statements

❏   INTERROGATIVE, for asking questions

❏   IMPERATIVE, for giving orders and making requests

❏   EXCLAMATIVE, for making exclamations.

sentence adverbial
61–63
92–93

CONJUNCTS and DISJUNCTS are described as sentence adverbials. They help to provide links between different parts of a text.

sentence types
97–98

There are four sentence types, as described above under 'sentences'.

simple aspect
78

The verb phrase can have three aspects; simple, CONTINUOUS, and PERFECT. The continuous and perfect aspects provide a particular comment on the action referred to by the verb. The simple aspect is 'unmarked' and makes no particular comment.

See SIMPLE FUTURE, SIMPLE PAST, SIMPLE PRESENT.

simple future tense
77

The tense formed by using *will* or *shall* followed by the VERB STEM. It is used to refer to:

❏   plans or commitments
*We **shall visit** brother Rizla at the monastery.*

❏   predictions
*The new laws **will be** a disaster.*

❏   ability or capacity
*This diet **will work** for men and women just as effectively.*

❏   habits
*And even when you think you know the island intimately it **will keep on springing** surprises.*

simple past tense
77

In REGULAR verbs the simple past is formed by adding *-ed* to the VERB STEM. In IRREGULAR verbs it is formed in a variety of ways. It is used to refer to:

❏   a single event in the past
*One of the boys **tripped** over and **crashed** into a tree.*

❑ a series of repeated events in the past
*He **taught** once a week in the primary school.*

simple present
77

The simple present tense is formed from the STEM of the VERB and -*s* is added for the THIRD PERSON SINGULAR, *he/she/it*:

*She **works** at Crompton's, on the industrial estate.*

This tense has a wide variety of uses. Among others, it is used to refer to:

❑ habitual actions
*Once a week farmers **gather** in their local market town.*

❑ present thoughts and feelings
*He **believes** all his accidents are due to a cosmic conspiracy.*

❑ actions or states that are true now but have gone on for some time and may well go on in the future
*He **works** for Cadogan's, the art dealers.*

❑ timeless truths
*Water **boils** at 100°C at one atmosphere pressure.*

❑ planned or scheduled events
*Three days later they **visit** Prenton Park to meet Tranmere.*

❑ open conditionals
*I'll be at my desk if you **phone**.*

simple sentence

A SENTENCE that contains one CLAUSE.

singular
47

Most NOUNS and many PRONOUNS have singular and PLURAL forms. The singular is used when there is only one person, thing, or idea referred to. If the SUBJECT of a CLAUSE is singular, the VERB must agree with it.

stem
25–26

The form of a word to which additional parts can be added. In this book the word 'stem' is used in two ways:

❑ to refer to the base form of a VERB, for example *walk*, which is then used to form TENSES and PARTICIPLES

❑ to refer to the base form of any word to which PREFIXES and SUFFIXES are added to form new words.

subject   A CLAUSE ELEMENT. Usually in a statement the subject:
8–9
87, 95   ❑   comes at or near the beginning of the CLAUSE

                ❑   comes before the VERB

                ❑   is a NOUN, A PRONOUN, or A NOUN PHRASE

                ❑   often gives a good idea of what the sentence is
                    going to be about.

subject complement   A CLAUSE ELEMENT. As the name suggests, it completes
12–13   the meaning of the SUBJECT in clauses that follow the
90, 95   pattern: SUBJECT + VERB + COMPLEMENT:

                *Sportswear is **the new influence on high fashion**.*

                *She seems **rather charming**.*

                As these examples show, the subject complement can
                be a NOUN or NOUN PHRASE, or an ADJECTIVE or ADJECTIVE
                PHRASE. It can also be a PRONOUN.

subordinate clause   In a COMPLEX SENTENCE a subordinate clause serves as a
40, 101–104   CLAUSE ELEMENT to the MAIN CLAUSE. Subordinate clauses
                can be:

                ❑   SUBJECT
                    What we are offering *is valuable.*

                ❑   OBJECT
                    *Do you know **what they have done there**?*

                ❑   SUBJECT COMPLEMENT
                    *Diversity is **what he has sought all his life.***

                ❑   OBJECT COMPLEMENT
                    *And it was, after all, his science that made him **what
                    he was**.*

                ❑   ADVERBIAL
                    ***After they had gone**, the others sat round the table
                    and discussed them.*

subordinating   A CONJUNCTION that introduces a SUBORDINATE
conjunction   CLAUSE. In the examples that follow the subordinating
42, 69–70   conjunctions are in bold type:

                ***When** I arrived home, I sat down at my desk and
                wrote a letter.*

*She was in control now, **because** she knew the truth about Simon's real character.*

*Even the players themselves are getting concerned **although** they put it in slightly different terms.*

suffix An AFFIX which is attached to the end of a STEM to form a new word. In the examples that follow the suffixes are in bold type.

*understand**able** beautif**ul** examin**ation***

superlative All QUALITATIVE ADJECTIVES have three forms:
23, 51–52

ABSOLUTE	COMPARATIVE	SUPERLATIVE
tall	*taller*	*tallest*
good	*better*	*best*
attractive	*more attractive*	*most attractive*

The SUPERLATIVE is used when three or more items are being compared:

*The **tallest** player in our side is not six foot!*

syntax The study of the ways in which words are organised into SENTENCES. Traditionally, GRAMMAR consists of syntax and MORPHOLOGY.

tag question A question 'tagged on' at the end of a SENTENCE. Tag questions are used, mainly in speech, when the speaker wishes the listener to confirm a statement. If the statement is positive, then the tag question is negative and vice versa:

*My word, our ancestors had some rare old times together, **didn't they?*** (Expected answer: *yes*)

*It's not too heavy for you to carry, **is it?*** (Expected answer: *no*)

Tag questions are formed using auxiliary verbs. If the verb phrase in the original statement contains an auxiliary verb, then that auxiliary is used to form the question, as in the second example. If the original statement does not contain an auxiliary, then a suitable auxiliary verb is used in the question, as in the first example.

tense
29–31, 77

In this book the grammatical term 'tense' is used in two ways. In the strictly grammatical sense English has two tenses: PRESENT and PAST. Grammatically a tense is a change in the form of a VERB, used to indicate time:

In his spare time Gavin **competes** *in various rallies.*

Nine pilots **competed***, the most for some years*

This definition is not useful, however, when you are trying to explain how English verbs work. The VERB PHRASE, which usually contains both MAIN VERBS (like *compete*) and AUXILIARY VERBS (like *is, had, will*) enables us to express a wide range of meanings relating to TIME and ASPECT. So the second way in which we can use the term 'tense' is to distinguish the following tenses in English:

	PRESENT	PAST	FUTURE
SIMPLE	*I see*	*I saw*	*I shall/will see*
CONTINUOUS	*I am seeing*	*I was seeing*	*I shall be seeing*
PERFECT	*I have seen*	*I had seen*	*I shall have seen*
PERFECT CONTINUOUS	*I have been seeing*	*I had been seeing*	*I shall have been seeing*

So in this broader sense, English has twelve tenses. While this may not satisfy strict grammarians, it makes life much easier for modern language teachers.

transitive verb
27, 54–55, 79

A VERB which is followed by an OBJECT:

Charlie Chaplin fans **are enjoying** *a revival in their hero's popularity.*

Verbs which do not require an object are described as INTRANSITIVE. Some verbs can be used both transitively and intransitively:

Only the tactics **have changed***.*

And George might easily **have changed** *his mind.*

uncountable noun   A NOUN which does not normally have a PLURAL,
17, 48, 67   sometimes called a MASS NOUN. Uncountable nouns
commonly refer to:

❏   things that are thought of in the mass rather than as
individual items
concrete   electricity   rain   mud

❏   abstract concepts
violence   beauty   fun   patience

You have to be careful, though. Many uncountables can
be counted in certain situations:

*He speculated on the bevy of **beauties** his mother
would line up next time.*

verb   The word 'verb' is used in two ways:
25–28
53–59   ❏   to refer to a WORD CLASS

❏   to refer to a CLAUSE ELEMENT
In this sense it is more properly described as the
VERB PHRASE.

As a word class, verbs are used:

❏   to refer to an action
*A mortar bomb **exploded** some distance away.*

❏   to refer to a state
*Jeanne **stayed** at home with her baby daughter.*

❏   to link a subject with its complement
*His future career then **seemed** uncertain.*

Verbs have the following forms:

STEM/INFINITIVE	*talk*	*run*	*go*
PRESENT PARTICIPLE	*talking*	*running*	*going*
PAST PARTICIPLE	*talked*	*run*	*gone*
PRESENT TENSE	*talk(s)*	*run(s)*	*go(es)*
PAST TENSE	*talked*	*ran*	*went*

See also: VERB PHRASE.

verb chain   An expression sometimes used to refer to the VERB PHRASE.

verb phrase
29–32
42–44
76–81

A CLAUSE ELEMENT. An essential part of a clause, the verb phrase consists of a MAIN VERB plus, optionally, one or more AUXILIARY VERBS. In a statement it normally comes after the SUBJECT:

SUBJECT	VERB PHRASE	REST OF SENTENCE
Dr Manorani	spoke	at a number of Amnesty meetings last autumn.
The owners	had expected	larger audiences.
She	would have liked to fall	in love with him.

verbal noun   See GERUND.

verbless clause
43–44

A clause which contains neither a finite nor a non-finite verb:

> *If possible, give a daytime telephone number.*

> *These are now on order and will be circulated **when available**.*

Verbless clauses can usually be expanded into full finite clauses:

> *If it is possible, give a daytime telephone number.*

> *These are now on order and will be circulated **when they are available**.*

voice
31–32
79–80

Clauses containing TRANSITIVE verbs can be ACTIVE or PASSIVE:

❑ active
Then you find out Tchaikovsky wrote it.

❑ passive
Then you find out it was written by Tchaikovsky.

Active and passive are referred to as 'voices'.

wh- question   Sometimes called 'open' questions, these invite a wide range of possible answers. They generally begin with one of the following:

who(m)	*whose*	*which*	*what*
why	*when*	*where*	*how*

word class
46–47

A group of words which perform similar grammatical jobs. Word classes can be divided into two:

❏ **open classes**
These are classes which are not limited in size, so new words continue to be added to them. They include NOUNS, VERBS, ADJECTIVES and ADVERBS.

❏ **closed classes**
These are the structure words used to connect open-class words together. They include PRONOUNS, PREPOSITIONS, CONJUNCTIONS, and DETERMINERS.

word family

A group of words each of which has a common STEM, to which are added different PREFIXES and SUFFIXES. For example, the stem *examine*, produces the following word family:

examinability	*examinable*	*examination*
examine	*examinee*	*examiner*
pre-examination	*pre-examine*	*re-examinable*
re-examination	*unexaminable*	

The structure of the family can be shown in a diagram like this:

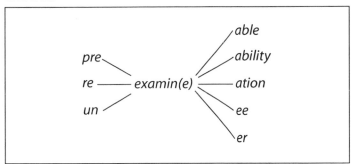

yes/no question

A question to which the speaker expects one of two answers, *yes* or *no*. It is contrasted with three other types of question:

❏ a *wh-* QUESTION, which leaves the possible answer open

❏ an *either/or* QUESTION, which provides two alternative answers

❑ a TAG QUESTION, which expects agreement or confirmation from the audience

zero relative Many RELATIVE CLAUSES are introduced by RELATIVE
74 PRONOUNS, such as *who* or *that*. However, it is also possible to have a relative clause that is not introduced by any relative pronoun:

*Animals always came first – every book **I read** was about them.*

In this situation it is said that the clause is introduced by a zero relative.

Further reading

The main books I have consulted while writing *Grammar for Teachers* are listed below. If you wish to explore grammar further, then I would recommend *The Oxford English Grammar* by Sidney Greenbaum as the simplest and clearest descriptive grammar. The *Collins Cobuild English Grammar* is the only one of the five not to take a descriptive approach. It is a functional grammar; that is to say that it looks at the different ways in which people wish to communicate and then shows how they use grammar to achieve this. For a teacher this approach is very useful. Like the other four titles, the Collins grammar is based on a corpus. It is clearly written and has good examples—once you have worked out how to find things in it.

Of the remaining titles, the Quirk grammar is the oldest, and by far the biggest. The Longman has a mass of useful statistical information about frequency. This is based on real usage rather than grammatical 'correctness'—a useful corrective. The *Cambridge Grammar* is the most recent and in many ways the most interesting. It contains all the material required in a straight descriptive grammar, but there is also a heavy emphasis on texts and communication, which comes as no surprise to those who know the work of Ron Carter. For teachers who are interested in applying grammatical insights to the teaching of writing, this is a very useful book.

The Oxford English Grammar, by Sidney Greenbaum
Oxford University Press, 1996 (ISBN 0-19-861250-8)

Collins Cobuild English Grammar, by John Sinclair
HarperCollins, latest edition 2005 (ISBN 0-00-718387-9)

Longman Grammar of Spoken and Written English, by Douglas Biber, Stig Johansson, Geoffrey Leech, Susan Conrad, and Edward Finegan
Pearson Education, 1999 (ISBN 0-582-23725-4)

A Comprehensive Grammar of the English Language, by Randolph Quirk, Sidney Greenbaum, Geoffrey Leech, Jan Svartvik
Longman, 1985 (ISBN 0-582-51634-6)

Cambridge Grammar of English, by Ronald Carter and Michael McCarthy
Cambridge University Press, 2006 (ISBN 0-521-58846-4)

Appendix: Grammar in the Primary Strategy

In England, the renewed Primary Strategy was published in 2006. The grammar is much less 'in your face' than it was in the older approach, but that does not mean that it is not there. The various documents that comprise the Strategy make use of just under sixty grammatical terms, which are listed below. Needless to say, they will all be found explained and cross-referenced in the Glossary.

Relevant Strategy Documents

The documents in which grammatical description and terminology are found are these:

- ❏ *Core learning in literacy by strand*
- ❏ *Developing reading comprehension*
- ❏ *Improving writing*
- ❏ *Progression in discussion texts*
- ❏ *Progression in explanatory texts*
- ❏ *Progression in instructional/procedural texts*
- ❏ *Progression in narrative*
- ❏ *Progression in non-chronological report*
- ❏ *Progression in persuasion texts*
- ❏ *Progression in poetry*
- ❏ *Progression in recount*

The grammatical terms used

The following grammatical terms are to be found in those documents:

abstract noun	countable	noun
adjectival phrase	determiner	passive
adjective	embedded clause	past
adverbial	grammar	past tense
adverbial phrase	grapheme	person
agreement	homophone	phoneme
clause	imperative	phrase
complex sentence	inflection	plural
compound sen-	inversion	possession
tence	lexical	prefix
conditional	metalinguistic	preposition
conjunction	modal	present
connective	morphology	present tense

pronoun	singular	uncountable
relative clause	subordinate	verb
root	subordinate clause	voice
sentence	subordination	word class
simple present	suffix	word family
tense	syntax	
simple sentence	tense	

There are two terms used in the strategy which are ambiguous, and which will not be found in the Glossary of the present book.

❑ **Adverbial phrase**
This is used to refer to a phrase which functions like an adverbial. This is slightly confusing because the Strategy also refers to 'adverbials'. In the Glossary, and throughout this book, a clear distinction is made between two related but different grammatical concepts: **adverbial** and **adverb phrase**. The distinction between the two is explained on pages 33-36.

❑ **Adjectival phrase**
It is not clear from the Strategy documents whether this means a phrase built up on an adjective, or a phrase used like an adjective. So it is advisable to stick to whichever of the following terms actually applies:

- adjective phrase
- premodifier
- postmodifier
- subject complement
- object complement

Connectives

This word has no grammatical standing but it is used a lot in the Strategy, so what follows is an attempt to explain its meanings and applications.

The Strategy talks about the use of connectives for the following purposes:

❑ **to provide information about time, place, manner, reason**
In this book, grammatical elements that do this are referred to as **adjuncts** and **conjunctions**.

❑ to provide cohesive links showing the semantic connec-
   tions between sentences
   In this book these are called **conjuncts**.

The lists that follow provide some of the simpler and more common adjuncts, conjunctions, and conjuncts.

Adjuncts and conjunctions

Time
Adjuncts

Single words
*afterwards, always, finally, hourly/monthly etc, never, next,
normally, often, once/twice etc, rarely, seldom, sometimes, then,
today, usually, yesterday*

Groups of words
*every week/month etc, last week/month etc, next week/month etc,
once/twice/three times a day/week etc, one day/year etc, sooner or
later*

Prepositional phrases beginning/using:
after, at, before, for, from...to, in, on, since, to, until/till

Time conjunctions

after, as, before, since, until/till, when, while

Place
Adjuncts

Place is commonly expressed by using prepositional phrases
such as *on the ground.*

Prepositions

The following prepositions are commonly used to form prepositional phrases indicating position:

*above, across, along, among, around, at, behind, below, beside,
between, down, in, in front of, near (to), off, on, on top of, opposite,
outside, through, under(neath), up, upon*

The following prepositions are commonly used to form prepositional phrases indicating direction:

along, around, down, from, into, off, onto, round, to, towards, up

There are also a number of adverbs which are used for this purpose:

backwards, down, forwards, here, in, out, sideways, there, up

Manner
The easiest way of saying how an action is performed is to use an
adverb of manner. Most of these are formed by adding the prefix
-ly to a suitable adjective. For example:

smooth   smoothly

Reason
Reason is most frequently expressed by using an adverbial clause
of reason. These are usually introduced by the subordinating
conjunctions:

because, since, as

Reason can also be expressed using a prepositional phrase beginning with *because of* or *owing to*.

Using conjuncts

Conjuncts are used to show the links between sentences. They
can be used to show a variety of different types of link. The commonest are:

Adding information

also, as well, besides, too

Showing cause

so, therefore, thus

Making a contrast

all the same, even so, however, though

Putting things in order

first(ly), finally, lastly, then

Constructing a narrative sequence

*afterwards, at the same time, earlier, finally, first, later, meanwhile,
next, presently, soon (after), suddenly, then*

Index

A

absolute 23, 51–52, 106
abstract noun. *See* noun
adjective 22–24, 50–52, 106
  attributive 22, 50, 110
  classifying 22–24, 51, 112
  predicative 22, 50, 139
  qualitative 22–24, 51, 144
adjective phrase. *See* phrase
adjunct 35–36, 61–62, 92–94, 107.
    See also adverb; adverbial
  focus 123
adverb 33–38, 60–63, 107
  relative 74, 144
adverbial 14–16, 31, 33–38, 61–63,
    92–94, 108
  sentence 146
adverbial clause. *See* clause
adverb phrase. *See* phrase
affix 109. *See also* word family
agreement 9, 58, 109
apposition 109
article 110. *See also* determiner
aspect 29–30, 77–78, 110
  continuous 78, 118–119
  perfect 78, 136
  simple 78, 146
attributive adjective. *See* adjective
auxiliary verb. *See* verb

B

backshift 111

C

cardinal numeral 111. *See also* determiner
case 111
  possessive 138
classifying adjective. *See* adjective
clause 6, 86–96, 112.
    See also clause patterns
  adverbial 41–42, 102–104, 108

  concession 116
  conditional 116
  conditional 103–104
  main 41, 100, 129
  nominal 41, 102, 131
  non-finite 43, 132
  relative 41, 73–75, 101–102, 144–145
    non-restrictive 101–102, 132
    restrictive 101–102, 145
  subordinate 41, 101–104, 148–149
  verbless 43–44, 152
clause element 86–94, 112–113
clause patterns 8–16, 95–96, 113
co-ordinating conjunction.
    See conjunction
collective noun. *See* noun
common noun. *See* noun
comparative 23, 51–52, 114.
    See also adjective
complement 114
  object 13, 90–91, 95, 134
  subject 12–13, 90, 95, 148
complex sentence. *See* sentence
compound sentence. *See* sentence
compound word 116
concord. *See* agreement
conditional 116
conjunct 36, 61–63, 92–93, 117.
    See also adverb; adverbial
conjunction 69, 118
  co-ordinating 40, 69, 119
  subordinating 42, 69–70, 149
connective 63, 118, 157–159
continuous aspect. *See* aspect
copular verb. *See* linking verb
countable noun. *See* noun

D

declarative 7, 87–88, 97, 120
determiner 20–21, 67, 120

Lightning Source UK Ltd.
Milton Keynes UK
28 September 2009

144267UK00001B/23/A